CODEBREAKING
SISTERS
Our Secret War

CODEBREAKING SISTERS

Our Secret War

Patricia and Jean Owtram

with Chris Manby

MIRROR BOOKS

First published by Mirror Books in 2020

Mirror Books is part of Reach plc
10 Lower Thames Street
London EC3R 6EN

www.mirrorbooks.co.uk

ISBN 978-1-913406-05-9

Typeset by Danny Lyle

Printed and bound in Great Britain by
CPI Group (UK) Ltd, Croydon, CR0 4YY

A CIP catalogue record for this book is available from the British Library.

Every effort has been made to fulfil requirements with regard to
reproducing copyright material. The author and publisher will be
glad to rectify any omissions at the earliest opportunity.

1 3 5 7 9 10 8 6 4 2

Cover images: Shutterstock / visitkent.co.uk

To the memory of our parents, Dorothy and Cary, our brother Robert, and our husbands Ray Davies and Michael Argles, who in their lifetimes did so much to make our lives happy and interesting.

When we were small children we had a nanny whom we called Beebee. Whenever we complained or cried about the trials of childhood, grazed knees and other mishaps, she cheered us up by making us say, "It might have been very much worse."

Years later, that phrase became a sort of mantra for us Owtram sisters. We still quote it to each other when things go wrong and it seldom fails to make us feel better. It is a sentiment that has helped to carry us through our darkest days. We had a happy childhood and we were especially lucky to have each other. Though we could not have guessed what lay ahead of us, our early days in Lancashire laid the foundation for two very interesting lives.

CHAPTER ONE

Patricia

I was born in 1923, five years after the end of the First World War. My sister Jean came along two years later. I had been told I would have a little brother or sister to play with so I was unimpressed when she arrived, telling our mother, "She's too little to be any use." Our brother Robert – Bobby – arrived five years after Jean.

We lived with our grandfather, Herbert Hawksworth Owtram, whom we called Grandboffin, in a house called Newland Hall near Dolphinholme, five miles from Lancaster. Our father, Cary Owtram, was just old enough to have been in the Royal Marines at the end of World War One. Our mother Dorothy, née Daniel, who was always known as Bunty, had been a land girl, driving a truck for the Women's Land Army. She was something of a trailblazer for her sex, having been one of the first women in Preston to gain a driving licence.

1

Grandboffin had invited our newly married parents to live with him at Newland Hall because our paternal grandmother had died in 1921. Our father was the second of four brothers and the younger two were still at school at the time. Naturally, the boys missed their mother terribly and so Grandboffin thought it would be much better if Cary and Bunty were there to make the house a happier home.

We think that the first Owtram to live at Newland Hall was our great-grandfather, who came from South Yorkshire. Newland was so named because it was *new* farming land, developed from previously wild moorland. The Owtram family had been in farming for generations but in the 19th century, our great-grandfather started working in the textile industry, travelling to France to buy fabric. Later he went into manufacturing. Our grandfather – Grandboffin – bought the first family mill, the Cliff Mill in Preston, where raw cotton was spun into yarn.

Grandboffin eventually sold the Cliff Mill and bought another spinning mill in Bolton. Each weekday morning of my childhood, Grandboffin and my father would take the local train there. I used to love going with them to visit. The mill throbbed with engines and was very noisy but it was also very warm. It was a welcome change from Newland Hall where our Aunt Gioia complained that the only warm room was the walk-in airing cupboard. Aunt Gioia was a novelist and when she came to stay, she would sometimes sit in the airing cupboard to write.

Newland Hall itself began life as a small farm house in the 18th century. Our great-grandfather added the dining room and kitchen. Grandboffin, who with four sons definitely needed extra space, added what became known as the billiard room wing. The house was built in local sandstone with a grey slate roof. It was surrounded by a large garden, designed by our great-grandmother, who was fond of rhododendrons, of which there were many. The family also planted a wood and had a stream dammed to create a lake, which was just big enough for us to have a rowing boat. There were two orchards and a cobbled stable yard. Meanwhile the barn had been converted into a garage and a former cattle shed had been given a proper floor for dances.

We were lucky to have such a big garden to play in as children. One of our favourite games was a sort of bicycle polo which we played on the lawn. Jean and I also loved to play "pretends". We had a dressing-up box full of dresses that had belonged to our grandmother and old uniforms handed down by the men of the family. We especially liked to play at being Jacobites, fighting the English. Having read about Bonnie Prince Charlie, Jean and I had developed an admiration for the Young Pretender. We used to write little plays and make Bobby dress up too.

There were always animals around the house. Our father and Grandboffin kept retrievers – spaniels and Labradors – but there was also a Dandie Dinmont called Meg and a Sealyham named Moogie. We had guinea pigs and budgies and for a while some bantam hens. Bobby had a long-suffering cat, called Tabitha, who spent most of her time avoiding the dogs. Then, one Christmas, our Great-Aunt Flo, who had married a millionaire, generously gave us a pony called Dolly. I was the first to ride Dolly in the field in front of the house. She threw me off within a minute and I twisted my ankle as I fell, but later Jean or I would come to ride her every day round the lanes, with Tommy Townson, a retired soldier who worked as Grandboffin's handyman and chauffeur, riding his bicycle alongside. Jean was a braver horsewoman than I was. She joined The Pony Club and took Dolly over small jumps!

As was common for families of our social class, nannies and governesses were a regular feature of our childhood. I didn't go to school until I was fourteen years old. Before then, I was educated at home with Jean or in the homes of local family friends who had governesses for their children too. I was an eager pupil. I learned to read at the age of four, encouraged by our mother and our nanny. Before I could write, I would make up poems that our mother transcribed for me. When I was still quite small, I wrote a poem based on the meter of Longfellow's "The Song of Hiawatha". It began,

"Thus the wild horse in his forest". Later, when I was about ten, I posted off a poem to the local paper. It was published. Much to my distress! When I saw the poem in print, I felt rather as though I had invaded my own privacy.

One of our first governesses, Miss Harrison, had been our mother's governess too. She was a little out of date when it came to teaching methods. While we went to dancing classes and had our posture corrected by being made to walk around with books balanced on our heads, Jean and I were taught no Latin or science. It was still the case that girls were just expected to grow up to get married and have children. However, we did get a grounding in English, history and the arts. Our mother drew beautifully so we learned to sketch through watching her. We were also lucky enough to be surrounded by books. We had all the classics and a great many of what one might have called "boys' books" that had belonged to our father and our uncles. I loved reading the works of Walter Scott. Dickens was a particular favourite too. I was always reading books considered "too old" for me and I couldn't wait to go away to boarding school.

Though Jean and I were educated at home, we weren't unaware of what was happening in the wider world. The family took *The Times* and the *Daily Mail* and I read both whenever I could. At the age of 13, in 1936, I was saddened by the news of Edward VIII's abdication to marry Mrs Wallis Simpson. Our Uncle Godfrey sang for our amusement, to the tune of the Christmas carol, "Hark the herald angels sing, Mrs Simpson stole our king".

As I headed into my teenage years there was gloomier news to digest. The papers carried coverage of the civil war that was raging in Spain. I was haunted by a photograph in the *Daily Mail*, which showed a man being executed by firing squad.

There had always been plenty of talk about the First World War in our family. Though he had been unable to go on active service, having broken his thigh bone as a young man, our grandfather was a colonel in the militia. Our Uncle Tom had been on the Western Front. Our father had joined the Royal Marines as soon as he was old enough, just in time for the last year of the war. Since then, Daddy had been in the Territorial Army. Meanwhile our mother's brother Charles, whom we called Uncle Tid, was in the Royal Navy. The wartime reminiscences of the older generation sounded so exciting that Jean and I felt we had just missed out on the greatest historical event of the century.

Sometimes the whole family would walk to a disused quarry nearby to play a game we called "bombing the Germans", inspired by our elders' First World War experiences. There was all sorts of rubbish in the quarry, including an old iron wheelbarrow. The aim was to hit that barrow, which represented the Germans, with rocks. If you got a direct hit, it made a very satisfying clang. The grown-ups let us play the game to our hearts' content until our young cousin Jill came to stay one summer. She brought with her a governess – a German governess – named Fräulein Fischer. Our childish hostilities against the Hun were called off while Fräulein Fischer was in residence.

As the 1930s went on, the news we read in the papers about Germany became more worrying. Germany was re-arming and we were not. All the same, I don't think I really expected that Britain would be at war again in my lifetime. I'd assumed that Jean, Bobby and I would live out our lives in blissful peace. The photograph from the civil war in Spain reminded me what a fragile thing peace can be.

CHAPTER TWO

Patricia

August 1939

Our father was a keen fisherman and was at his very happiest wherever he might catch a trout or a salmon. He taught the rest of us to fish as well and soon we were all hooked; thus Scotland, where the fishing was particularly good, was a popular holiday destination for the whole Owtram family.

In the August of 1939, shortly after I turned 16, we went as planned to the west of Scotland for our annual break. Previously we'd stayed in small hotels and guest houses but this time our father borrowed a caravan from our local GP, Dr Daniel. Daddy hitched it to our car and we drove north with much excitement. Our cousin Monica followed in her car. She was going to be staying in a tent. I'd just finished my school certificate and was looking forward to a family break before returning to boarding school at Wroxall Abbey near

Warwick, where Jean would be joining me for the first time in September. The weather was mostly beautiful, though of course, being Scotland, the air was full of midges and other tiny biting things that made a meal of us while we tried to catch something for dinner.

I was captivated by Arisaig, which I described in my diary of the time. *"Rocks, white sand, orange seaweed, seagulls, blue, green and purple sea, blue islands, Skye, Rum, Eigg"* As well as fishing we attended the Arisaig Games, where Cousin Monica and I were rather taken by the local laird and spent much of the day trying to catch his attention. One night we saw the Northern Lights. *"Great pulsing white rivers and pools of light all over the sky… Watched them for hours,"* my diary entry says for that day. It was idyllic.

However, all summer an increase in German aggression had been front-page news. Hitler had annexed Austria in 1938 and in March 1939, his forces had occupied Czechoslovakia. Now they had their sights set on Poland. We learned more from the daily bulletins on the radio. At home we had a radio of our own, but while we were camping near Fort William, the only way to hear the news was to go to the local farmhouse, where the farmer, Mr Macdonald, kindly welcomed us in so we could keep up to date on developments. Alas, the news was not good and one bulletin in particular convinced our father that he should cut the holiday short and return to his regiment forthwith. Another family camping nearby had already come to the same decision.

At this time, our father was a major in the 137th Field Regiment, Royal Artillery, which was based in Blackpool. He felt very strongly that he should be with his men when the news coming out of Eastern Europe was so bad. It seemed inevitable that Britain would be dragged into the situation at some point and no-one knew how quickly the troops would need to be ready.

"Heartbreaking," I told my diary, *"To leave all this undiluted peace and beauty."* But we were all resigned to ending our lovely trip early.

Unfortunately getting back from Scotland was not quite so simple as it might have been. The road from Fort William to our remote camping spot was being repaired and was so bumpy that upon our arrival we'd discovered that most of the crockery was smashed. Unwilling to risk more breakages on the way back – after all, it was a borrowed caravan – our father decided the only way to get back along that awful road safely was by lightening the load and putting the van on a tow truck. That meant jettisoning us three children and our luggage.

Our cousin Monica had already gone home so I was left in charge of Bobby and Jean. The idea was that we would take the train from Mallaig to Fort William and meet up with our parents there for the rest of the journey home, which would be on smoother roads.

Naturally, we children decided to make the whole thing into an adventure. We made a plan to leave our cases in the left luggage office at the Fort William train station and use the time we had there, waiting for our parents to arrive, to explore the lower reaches of Ben Nevis. We were all very excited at the thought. In the event, our plan was scuppered by an IRA security alert which meant that the left luggage office was closed (this was at the height of IRA's S-Plan or Sabotage Campaign – they had only recently killed five in a bomb attack on Coventry). Since we couldn't climb a mountain with our suitcases, all we could do was sit in the station waiting room.

We arrived home a couple of days later and our father went straight to join his regiment in Blackpool. After that, things happened very quickly. At dawn on 1 September 1939, Hitler launched the invasion of Poland that had been brewing for months. Though the Poles fought with great courage, they were at a disadvantage from the start, vastly outnumbered by the German troops and no match for the German war machinery. As Poland fell we knew there were implications for us too. Britain and France had promised to go to Poland's aid.

We were all of us, including Daddy, at Newland Hall on 3 September 1939, when we heard that Prime Minister Neville Chamberlain was going to make an announcement to the nation. It was a Sunday morning. We always went to St Mark's Church in Dolphinholme on Sundays. Our father was a church warden there. But the news of a radio announcement at eleven o'clock threw our usual plans into disarray. We understood that such an announcement was going to be serious and the whole village would stop to listen. Newland was at quite a distance from St Mark's, so having travelled there in anticipation of a service, we joined the vicar, Mr Jenkins, to listen to the news in the house of the Brennand family, who lived close by the church.

I will never forget hearing Prime Minister Chamberlain's words that day as he explained that Germany's invasion of Poland had left the United Kingdom with no choice but to declare war on Herr Hitler and his allies.

"We have a clear conscience. We have done all that any country could do to establish peace," he said. "But the situation in which no word given by Germany's ruler could be trusted, and no people or country could feel itself safe, had become intolerable. And now that we have resolved to finish it, I know that you will all play your part with calmness and courage."

The announcement left us children in a state of excitement. I think we expected the German bombers to arrive seconds after the radio was turned off. Our parents however were quiet and grave as they digested the news. They knew only too well what war really meant. France declared war on Germany the same day.

Chapter Two

That night, I wrote in my diary, *"WAR declared on Germany, no reply to ultimatum. PM very tired and discouraged. KING spoke at 6, labour leaders at 9.30. All fine speeches. Seems incredible, but I feel almost glad it has started after all these crises."*

CHAPTER THREE

Jean

I remember that summer holiday in Scotland very well. I was tremendously excited to be staying where my childhood heroes, the Jacobites, had lived and I was just as enthusiastic about fly fishing as our father was. It was a terrible pity to have to cut the trip short. But oh for what a reason!

When the war on Germany was declared, I'll admit that I thought it was terrific news. What an adventure it would be. Like Pat, as a young girl I'd envied our parents and their siblings the exciting time they seemed to have had in the First World War. I'd read lots of books that romanticised those years. This was going to be my generation's moment.

Of course I had no idea what a new war with Germany might actually entail. That Sunday, as our parents and Mr Jenkins the vicar discussed the situation, Pat and I were probably most excited at the prospect of getting out of going to church. However after some brief discussion, it was decided that the morning's service should go ahead. Now, more than ever, the congregation needed to be in God's presence. Mr Jenkins prayed for peace. Later the same day, a birthday party for Philip, a local boy who was turning seven, also went ahead as planned.

I was almost disappointed when, to begin with at least, absolutely nothing seemed to change. Pat and I were soon at school. I was joining her for the first time at Wroxall Abbey. After all those years of being taught at home by governesses, I'd been very much looking forward to going away at last, having read all the boarding school books I could lay my hands on while I was waiting. In some ways, for 14-year old me, going off to school in the September of 1939 was far more daunting than the thought of the country being at war.

Unfortunately school was immediately disillusioning. It was not the wild riot of midnight feasts I had been led to believe it would be and at first I also seemed to be quite unpopular. I think that perhaps because I was Patricia Owtram's little sister – Pat was deputy head girl by this time – people thought I might be benefitting from favouritism. Whatever the reason, it took me a while to find my niche and I suffered some bullying.

Of course, the war meant that things actually *were* a little different at the school from when Pat had joined two years earlier. For a start, we had all been given gas masks and we had a great many fire drills. In particular we had to practise using the fire escapes. This was more complicated than you might imagine.

My classroom was on the second floor of the school building but there was no ladder or outdoor staircase to climb down to safety. No, to escape the room in the event of a blaze, we would have to throw a long rope out of the window and shimmy down that. This was not as easy as it sounds, since one had to get down the rope without accidentally kicking a hole in the huge stained-glass window – Dame Alice's Window – on the floor below. There was nowhere safe to put one's feet. I suppose that in the case of an actual fire, no-one would have cared *too* much if the precious window got the odd kick or two but practices were fraught as the teachers stood in the gardens below and bellowed out warnings.

"Don't put your feet on the window, Jean!"

They had reason to worry. Pat remembers how her heart sank upon hearing me shout "First breakage!" after a terrible cacophony of shattering china and glass. I had somehow managed to knock over an entire wash stand, breaking both the porcelain basin and soap dish. Girls were allowed two accidental breakages of school property before their parents were expected to pay up, hence my shout, though I think that at the time the rule was initiated, the school probably envisaged a breakage as involving a single plate or cup. Not an entire wash-stand. If anyone was going to accidentally swing through Dame Alice's window, it would probably be me.

There was a similar fire escape arrangement at our brother Bobby's school, where one of the cooks was so traumatised by the experience of evacuating by rope (she got caught on a nail) that she handed in her notice halfway down.

At Wroxall Abbey we also had to practice for air raids. In the event of hearing the sirens, we would all hurry down into the cellars, which had been made over into music practice rooms when the Abbey became a school. I already spent a great deal of time in those "cells", as we called them. In the first instance, to practise playing the piano. In the second instance, because they were the perfect place to have a sneaky cigarette. They had vents which were very effective at taking the smoke outside to help an illicit smoker avoid detection by the teaching staff.

Things did eventually start to change at Newland Hall too. Our father's regiment was training in earnest, though during the autumn of 1939 he was still able to live at home and commute to Blackpool and later to the grounds of Lord Derby's house, Knowsley Hall near Liverpool, for practice manoeuvres. The 137th Field Regiment had to wait a frustratingly long time to get their guns, which were being made in France, before they could be sent to Salisbury Plain to complete their training there.

Down in London, our father's elder brother Tom was now at the War Office. Prior to 1939, he'd been a lawyer for Shell, the oil company. During the war his role would be to keep tabs on Hitler's oil supplies. The third Owtram brother, Godfrey, was the director of a number of chemical companies, which provided raw materials for the war effort, so as this was a reserved occupation he carried on as before. Our father's youngest brother, Bill, joined the Sherwood Foresters, a line infantry regiment based in Nottinghamshire. Our mother Bunty had just one brother, Charles Saumarez Daniel. When the war started, he was Captain of HMS Faulknor, a Royal Navy F-class destroyer, which became the first British destroyer to sink a German U-boat, the U-39, on 14 September.

Meanwhile, our mother agreed to take evacuees at Newland Hall when the time came and also became an ARP (Air Raid Precautions) warden. She had been a land girl in the First World War. Now she was responsible for making sure that the local householders were sticking to the strict blackout rules, which were designed to baffle enemy bomber pilots looking for a target by night (all the local signposts had been removed to foil the enemy by day). The villagers took the blackout seriously. Our mother usually found that the only illegal light she ever saw was escaping from the windows of our house!

But the person who threw himself into the war effort most whole-heartedly was our grandfather, Grandboffin.

Grandboffin was so called because our father and uncles' nickname for their bookish father had been "Boffin". We were fond of nicknames in our family. I was Jane or Jinks. Pat was Trix or Trisha. Robert was Bobby, Bob or, when we were being especially affectionate, Nitwit or Nit.

Though in previous conflicts Grandboffin had been unable to go to the front due to his damaged leg, and he was now in his mid-seventies in any case, he had always been a military-minded man and he soon set in action a plan to defend the family home from an enemy invasion.

Grandboffin had always more than lived up to the Owtram family motto, "Frangas, non flectes", which means "you may break me but you cannot bend me". Those words were included in the crest which was painted on the side of the car he'd had specially adapted to accommodate his bad leg. Never was there a moment when the family motto seemed more apt. Since the declaration of war, Grandboffin had kept his old militia uniform to hand and slept with his sword and pistol by the bed (he'd decided that he must be in uniform if he was going to shoot an enemy soldier). But that was just the start. When Pat and I were not at school, we were pressed to join his home army.

Grandboffin was convinced it was a matter of time before the Germans invaded and we needed to be ready for them when they did. He'd decided that they would most likely arrive by air, dropping down on parachutes. He persuaded Newland Hall's two farm hands, who were in their thirties, to build sentry posts outside the back gate, one on either side of the road, which they would man when the invaders came. The gardener claimed he was exempt from war duties as an essential food producer. The rest of us had no such excuses. We were enlisted. Grandboffin was determined that the Germans would not find Newland Hall an easy target.

CHAPTER FOUR

Patricia

Though I had seen plenty of game shoots as a child, I had never actually held a gun. Girls weren't encouraged to shoot and I had never wanted to. I certainly didn't want to fire at a living creature. Now however, as part of Grandboffin's war plan, I was going to have to learn how. I had to join our mother and the other women of the house for regular rifle training in the garden. Grandboffin set up a cardboard target in the azalea bed and had us lie on our stomachs, sniper-style, behind a low wall to take shots at it.

Once I got used to handling a rook rifle, my aim quickly improved and I almost started to look forward to Grandboffin's drills. Jean, who would have been a good shot, I'm sure, was somewhat put out that she wasn't included in Grandboffin's family artillery, but she had an equally important task. If not *more* important. At the first sighting of an enemy paratrooper

21

floating down into the grounds of the house, Jean was to gather up our little brother Bobby and take him from Newland Hall to the tenant farm next door, where Grandboffin had decided the son and heir would be much safer. Jean took some convincing that hers was a vital role.

As befitted its size, Newland Hall once had a fairly large domestic staff to attend to its day-to-day running. That number had been cut back by the 1930s but our grandfather still insisted we needed a cook and a housemaid as well as the gardener and the farm hands. However, it had become increasingly difficult to find people who were willing to go into service in a big house in the middle of the countryside. Having had no luck recruiting locally, Grandboffin turned to a recruitment agency in London, which specialised in finding work for newly arrived Jewish Austrians, who had been forced to leave their homes by the rise of the Nazis in mainland Europe.

Among the Austrians who came to Newland Hall at this time was a young woman called Edith Krochmalnik. Soon after she arrived, she encouraged her schoolfriend, Cecelie Getzl – known to all as Lilly – to come and join her. Lilly came from a well-to-do Viennese family. She had relations by marriage in the United States and had hoped to join them there, but the outbreak of war prevented her from travelling onwards from England. Lilly was in her late 20s when she arrived at Newland Hall and joined Edith in the kitchen, while she considered her next move. Our mother, perhaps recognising a kindred spirit, did her best to make Lilly comfortable. The villagers too were welcoming, though after war was officially declared, the local policeman did have to interview Lilly and Edith to make sure they weren't enemy agents hiding in plain sight. After a strange conversation in which he asked Edith whether she was in the habit of shooting rabbits, she and Lilly were allowed to go about their business. Which included being part of Grandboffin's rifles.

There wasn't much to do in the evenings at Newland so Jean and I often found ourselves sitting in the warmth of the maids' parlour next to the kitchen, listening to Lilly's stories. Somehow, when the first of our grandfather's Austrian recruits arrived, I found myself cast as Newland Hall's chief interpreter. My first job was to label the taps in the kitchen. There were two sources of water to the house. One came from the mains, the other from a spring, which was thought to taste better. Grandboffin wanted the spring water taps to be labelled as drinking water. Armed with an English-German dictionary that had belonged to one of my uncles, I carefully wrote out "Wasser für trinken" on cardboard luggage labels. That was where my education in the German language began.

Lilly spoke hardly any English when first she arrived in Lancashire and I certainly spoke hardly any German but with Lilly's help, I soon became quite fluent. The kitchen chat was always more in German than in English. She let Jean and me read her Austrian magazines and letters from her sister in Hungary too. I remember being struck by how different Lilly's sister's handwriting looked from the English handwriting I was used to.

Lilly often regaled us with stories about her former life in Vienna, the glittering social scene and the fabulous concerts and operas she'd attended. She came from a musical family. One of her nephews was a talented violinist. Both Jean and I were fascinated to hear that in Vienna the dialling tone of all the telephones was set to a perfect "A" for the purpose of tuning instruments. The idea of such a cultured city was enthralling.

My sister and I were also very interested in hearing about Viennese food. When Lilly first arrived, her cooking seemed wonderfully exotic and Jean and I greatly enjoyed her different ways of preparing the same old vegetables. Her delicious Wiener Torte was very special. Unfortunately, Grandboffin was less enthusiastic and wanted nothing but classic English cooking coming out of his kitchen and Lilly soon adjusted her repertoire to suit Grandboffin's English taste.

Being stuck in isolation at Newland Hall, where one had to walk a quarter of a mile to the crossroads to catch a bus to Lancaster, could not have been more different from the cosmopolitan Viennese city life, I'm sure. The Vienna that Edith and Lilly had left behind sounded terribly exciting and Jean and I longed to go there. All the same, we had no idea how important those evenings spent talking German in the kitchen would turn out to be.

After the declaration of war, I'd returned to school to study for my higher certificate but I couldn't really see the point of it any more, particularly as I spent the best part of the spring term in the school sanitorium. Hearing the news every day, I was desperate to be doing my own bit for the war effort. It took much negotiating but I finally managed to persuade my parents to let me leave school after just two terms instead of the three we'd previously agreed. I left at Easter. I was 17 years old.

I first tried to get a job as an ambulance driver but was quickly turned down on the grounds of my age, so I planned to join the WAAF – the Women's Auxiliary Air Force – as soon as I turned 18. My options until I could sign up were not terribly exciting. I couldn't go to university. Jean and I had long been made to understand that privilege was reserved for Bobby, the son and heir, alone. It would have been too expensive to send us girls as well. Instead, we could choose between domestic science school or secretarial college. I chose secretarial college, thinking that perhaps it would be more useful for the career I hoped to have once the war was over. An English teacher at Wroxall Abbey had dismissed one of my essays as "journalese". She hadn't meant it to be a compliment but she'd unwittingly encouraged me to set my sights on being a journalist.

CHAPTER FIVE

Jean

After the Easter holidays of 1940, I returned to Wroxall Abbey without Pat. Perhaps because I was out of Pat's shadow, I started to enjoy school much more. I was good at sport and played on all the first teams for hockey, lacrosse and the like. That lent an automatic degree of popularity. As did playing the piano for all the school events and dances. But though in Pat's absence my popularity seemed increased, I missed having her there for our private conversations about the problems and successes of our school life.

Life at Wroxall Abbey was the epitome of "Keep calm and carry on" that year. As it was the summer term, we played tennis and cricket. Though for the moment we were unable to go to the theatre in Stratford to watch Shakespeare as Pat's class had done, we were visited by the Osiris Players Repertory Company, who performed G.B. Shaw's *St Joan*. I was very struck by the play, though shocked by Shaw's hostility to religion. Like my parents, I myself had a strong faith. On Sunday mornings, I would cycle from school to a church in the nearby village of Lapworth for the early service.

When we girls had spare time, we would knit socks to send to our troops on the front line. I don't think I had a natural talent for knitting. My letters home charted the progress of my attempt at a sock inch by painstaking inch over weeks. Several of my socks were retained as being much too small for any soldier's feet.

That summer term there were no air raids anywhere near Wroxall Abbey, but many of my classmates had heard the sirens in other places and some parents were taking drastic precautions to ensure their children's safety. Several girls were removed from school. One of my classmates was sent to live with her sister in Canada for the duration of the conflict. Another class, having just been moved to a bigger room to accommodate it, suddenly shrank to just six pupils. I wondered if the parents of the disappearing girls were over-reacting.

At half-term and on exeat, I returned to Newland Hall, where our mother and Grandboffin were holding the fort while our father was training with his regiment on Salisbury Plain. Grandboffin was glad to have me around. He and I had always been close. Prior to the war, our family had adhered to the social etiquette of the time which meant that, as the elder daughter, it was Pat's privilege to accompany our mother on her social visits. Pat loved to join Mama on her calls, hoping for the moment when a hostess might invite her to look around the private rooms of the house and even, perhaps, to take a peek in the wardrobe. Pat loved to see the ladies' formal dresses.

While Pat was with our mother, I was usually left at home with Grandboffin, who made no allowances at all for the fact that I was a girl. Even when I was quite small, he talked to me of farming and cattle as though I was an adult man. He kept a herd of pedigree shorthorn cows, of which he was immensely proud, and I soon learned all about them. I loved to see the newborn calves and to accompany Grandboffin to the agricultural shows where he entered his best cows in competition. When I was big enough, I was allowed to walk the cows around the show ring myself. I remember how I swelled with pride when I heard Grandboffin tell one of his friends, "Look at her shoulders. She's going to be a farmer." It was everything I wanted at the time.

But back from school, with our father away at training camp on Salisbury Plain and the war gathering pace, I was starting to find cataloguing the long pedigrees of Grandboffin's herd slightly less exciting than I once had. I wondered if the war would still be happening by the time I left school and if I could actually play a part.

In the late spring of 1940, on 10 May, Hitler had invaded Belgium and Holland, which up until that point had been neutral. That same day, Winston Churchill had become Prime Minister of the United Kingdom, following Neville Chamberlain's resignation. Everybody hoped that Churchill would turn the war around. Chamberlain had lost the support of his party – and much of the country too – after British troops had failed to prevent the German occupation of Norway back in April. Chamberlain was blamed for the disaster. As a family, we had a special connection to Norway. Pat's godmother Aunt Eleanor's husband, Sir Laurence Collier, had been appointed the British Ambassador to the Court of Norway. The Norwegian King, Haakon VII, had escaped the country and set up his court in exile in London.

All over Europe Hitler's troops were making efficient progress. Holland was able to hold out against the German forces for just five days. Belgium surrendered on 28 May. As the Germans made inroads into Northern France, the British Expeditionary Force, which was supporting the French troops there, was suddenly in grave danger.

An evacuation had to be organised. It would become possibly the most famous evacuation in the history of war. Over a period of nine days at the end of May and beginning of June 1940, the Royal Navy and its French equivalent, supported by thousands of small civilian vessels that set out from the Thames and from fishing villages all along the south and east coast, were able to evacuate more than 300,000 British and French troops from Dunkirk. It was an incredible feat of bravery and daring in the face of terrible danger.

By the beginning of June, some politicians, such as Lord Halifax the foreign secretary, had been discussing the possibility of negotiating with the Germans, but the overwhelmingly positive public response to the heroic efforts of both the forces and civilians at Dunkirk gave Winston Churchill the renewed support he needed to resist the calls for appeasement and fight on.

We all thought the world of Winston Churchill. He was a tremendous leader. His stirring words took the sting out of the humiliation of the retreat from Dunkirk and reminded us that there was still everything to fight for.

Of course the newspapers were full of reports from Dunkirk but we heard the details first-hand in Dolphinholme from the vicar's son, Ronald Jenkins, who was part of an army regiment that had been evacuated. He came to Newland Hall to tell us all about it. Pat, Bobby and I were desperately eager to hear everything but poor Ronald had to wait until our grandfather had finished listening to the fat stock prices on the radio before he could begin his story. Grandboffin's short-horn cows still came before any tales of wartime adventure.

I remember listening to Churchill's famous speech about Dunkirk on 4 June 1940.

"Even though large tracts of Europe and many old and famous States have fallen or may fall into the grip of the Gestapo and all the odious apparatus of Nazi rule, we shall not flag or fail. We shall go on to the end, we shall fight in France, we shall fight on the seas and oceans, we shall fight with growing confidence and growing strength in the air, we shall defend our Island, whatever the cost may be, we shall fight on the beaches, we shall fight on the landing grounds, we shall fight in the fields and in the streets, we shall fight in the hills; we shall never surrender, and even if, which I do not for a moment believe, this Island or a large part of it were subjugated and starving, then our Empire beyond the seas, armed and guarded by the British Fleet, would carry on the struggle, until, in God's good time, the New World, with all its power and might, steps forth to the rescue and the liberation of the old."

Later that same summer, the Germans occupied France and it seemed that Hitler had Britain in his sights at last. But to be able to invade our island nation, the Germans would have to deal with the Royal Air Force first. The war took to the air in earnest.

As the Luftwaffe aimed attacks at RAF airfields and aircraft factories, Lord Beaverbrook, Churchill's Minister of Aircraft Production, commanded that the manufacture of our iconic fighter planes – the Hurricanes and the Spitfires

– be stepped up. What would become known as the *Battle of Britain* began with the Luftwaffe targeting shipping convoys and ports such as Portsmouth before they shifted their focus to RAF airfields and factories.

However, by bringing the fight over British soil, the Germans had put themselves at a disadvantage. When one of our pilots was shot down, he would land among friends and soon be back in the sky again. When a German pilot was shot down over Britain, he would be taken straight to a prisoner of war camp and thus be out of action whether he was injured or not. When it was clear they were making less headway than they expected, the Luftwaffe began to target civilians in an attempt to lower morale, and *The Battle of Britain* gave way to the terror of *The Blitz*.

Returning to school for the autumn term of 1940, those girls who remained at Wroxall Abbey could not pretend that the War was not happening anymore. The school was just 10 miles away from Coventry, which, due to its importance as a manufacturing base, was an obvious target for the Luftwaffe. As the Battle of Britain escalated, Coventry suffered several raids and we were kept under rather stricter control than before. We were no longer allowed to stray outside the school garden without supervision. Fire drills happened more and more often. Some of the older pupils were put on a nightly fire watch rota.

I was at school on 14 November 1940, when Coventry was directly targeted in a raid that the Germans called "Operation Mondschiensonate" (Moonlight Sonata) because it was planned for the night of the full moon. We saw the German bombers fly overhead and minutes later, from the safety of the music rooms in the school's cellars, we heard the noise of the bombs as they exploded. More than 500 German bombers were involved in all, dropping both high explosive and incendiary bombs. Our anti-aircraft guns were able to bring down only one German plane.

The attack went on into the morning of 15 November. Once the all-clear had sounded and we were allowed back upstairs, we could see a sinister orange glow on the horizon. Coventry was ablaze. We also discovered that a German bomber returning from its sortie had dropped a landmine right outside the school gates.

A few days later, I wrote to my mother. "*Poor Coventry got it very badly last Thursday night. It was an amazing sight and the noise was pretty bad. The moon was full and the sky over Coventry was orange and smokey, instead of just moonlit. There were lots of parachutes, flares and rockets (to warn the AA guns that our planes were up)… One bomb landed about 500-600 yards away in a field. Of course, we all woke up and waited for the roof to fall in! But the ground was so soft that not even the windows burst on that side of the house.*"

The letter continues with talk of our plans for the Christmas holidays ahead. Despite what I'd seen, I remained quite blithe. However, there were many girls at the school whose families lived in Coventry. How must they have felt knowing their loved ones were in that burning city as we watched from our safe distance? Over 4,000 homes were destroyed, along with a third of the city's factories and, perhaps most devastating to morale, the city's cathedral had been set ablaze. More than 550 people were killed.

As we learned the full extent of the devastation, I did my best to tone down my excitement and offer them support. At the declaration of the war, I had longed for such adventure, but now I was beginning to understand how serious the conflict really was.

CHAPTER SIX

Patricia

Late 1940

In the autumn of 1940, I enrolled at the Triangle Secretarial College. For many years, the college had been on South Molton Street in central London, but now that the city was under nightly attack from the Luftwaffe, it had relocated to Gerrards Cross in South Buckinghamshire for safety. The Germans would have no reason to bomb leafy Gerrards Cross, where nothing much seemed to happen even in wartime.

Ironically, on the day I first arrived there, just as the housekeeper was showing me to what was to be my room for the next few months, something did happen. Something very dramatic indeed. As the housekeeper explained the rules of my new lodgings, we were suddenly thrown to the floor by an enormous explosion. The glass in the window bulged inwards, as though it was a giant soap bubble, before it shattered into thousands of pieces. The housekeeper and I immediately dived under the bed for safety and stayed there for quite some time, trying not to shake.

When we were finally sure it was safe to come out again, we discovered that a German mine had landed in the garden. It was a monster, weighing 500 pounds. Since Gerrards Cross wasn't an obvious target, a Luftwaffe plane must have dropped it on the way back from bombing nearby Slough, where there were factories making munitions and aircraft parts. The mine had quietly floated down onto the college's lawn on a parachute of fine knitted green silk before blowing the window in as it detonated on impact. I later found a scrap of the parachute fabric in the garden and for many years I kept it in an envelope marked with the time and date – 8.20pm, Saturday 28 September 1940 – along with a piece of shrapnel as big as my thumb. I kept it for luck. I would not have been so lucky had that piece of shrapnel hit me with any velocity. It was large enough to kill a man.

Such an inauspicious welcome to Gerrards Cross might have put some people off but I simply helped to clear up the broken glass and spent my first night in a different room. When I wrote to tell my parents that I was safely installed at the college, I decided against telling them what had really happened within an hour of my getting there. It had taken quite some effort to persuade my mother to allow me to leave school and travel down to Berkshire at the height of the Blitz. I didn't want to give her any reason to insist I was called straight back home. This was my first taste of real freedom. In any case, despite the explosion, I actually felt pretty safe at the Triangle College (though I didn't like the cellar where we had to sit out any air-raids. The hot water pipes went directly overhead, which was disconcerting). Outside, there were troops posted in the woods all around the house. I have no idea what those soldiers were really guarding, but they made us feel secure.

In class, we were taught shorthand, book-keeping and, of course, how to use a typewriter. We practised typing to the tune of "You are my sunshine" by Jimmie Davis and Charles Mitchell, which had the perfect rhythm. Though I'd taken piano lessons at school, I wasn't particularly musical, preferring to draw and paint instead, but I was soon tapping along to that song, improving my WPM speed every day.

Meanwhile my social life consisted mostly of going to the pictures in Gerrards Cross centre. I was a big film fan. Up until the age of 14, I had only seen four films, including *Tom Sawyer and Huckleberry Finn*, but it had been enough to get me hooked on the experience of going to the cinema whenever I could now I was an adult. I bought every film magazine I could lay my hands on and pored over the pictures of the big stars. The Austrian-born actress Hedy Lamarr with her cool blue eyes and wavy black hair was a particular favourite of mine. I also loved Laurence Olivier and Vivien Leigh, Leslie Howard as the *Scarlet Pimpernel* and Victor Mature.

On days off, I travelled into London on the Green Line coach. There I met up with family – my father would sometimes travel up from Salisbury Plain to meet me, or invite me to his base for dances – and friends including Gwen Webb Peploe, who was a girlhood friend of my mother's. In February 1941, I was invited to tea with Gwen, who was staying with a friend in Kensington. They were desperately trying to keep up appearances despite the bombing. I sent back this report to Newland Hall.

St Hubert's,
Gerrards Cross,
2nd February, 1941

My own darling Mum,

... dashed in a S.W. direction to Egerton Gardens, which is a red-brick street, as yet intact. One slight problem that had perplexed me a little, which was that I knew my hostess only as "Lady Winifred", was removed by finding a card with her full name on it jammed behind the bell.

Having no idea how one pronounced Lady W's surname, I asked for Gwen... Gwen appeared and we went into a room where Gwen quite unnecessarily did up her face and told me an endless saga about bronchitis and housemaids and flu and cooks and gastric trouble and parlour maids, all of which you will hear next week so I need not repeat it, and I gained the impression that I could hardly have come to tea less opportunely. However, the hum of tea eventually approached – it really was rather funny.

There was a square trapdoor in the corner of the floor through which, from time to time, appeared a lift. Somewhere below was a fierce Irish cook, whom one summoned by hammering on the floor with the fire-irons, simultaneously yelling, "Mrs Geary! Mrs Geeeeary!" The reply was an indignant Celtic shout, and one then shouted down messages such as, "Mrs Geary! You've sent up a completely empty tea-pot. We want one pink teapot with four teaspoonfuls of tea in it. Yes, three. No, listen Mrs Geary – can't you hear me? I said three. Oh, and if Mrs Allan hasn't gone yet, her ladyship wishes her to come up. And will you cut some bread-and-butter please. And don't forget the pink teapot with four teaspoonfuls –" etc. Gwen acted as diplomatic negotiator, and really, I don't altogether wonder that they have difficulty in keeping servants. All the same, I saw at least 3 different unwilling women about the house, and was told of yet another who had left before breakfast. Lady W improved on acquaintance, and would probably be a charming woman under normal conditions. I left fairly early, which may not entirely surprise you, at the same moment as a mournful woman who was demanding a week's wages while explaining that she had no time to do up anything for dinner etc. By the way – do destroy this letter before Gwen reaches Newlands!

I suppose this invasion will come off some time. I hope we will crush the horrors once and for all. Daddy seems to think so, and that if they do use gas it won't be the lethal kind, only mustard, which is cheering. People down here are extremely confident, but oh gosh, the tube-shelter children...

A few days later, I wrote to my mother again. This time with news of a new friend.

St Hubert's, Gerrards Cross, Bucks
23rd February, 1941

My own darling Mum,

It was lovely to get your last letter. I do love hearing from you. Would you terribly much mind if I didn't come home if there is an invasion? I would hate to run away while everyone else stayed put, and being at home in an invasion would be much more nightmarish than living somewhere one didn't care about. Also, all my life I should feel I had run away from it. I did discuss it with Daddy when we met a month ago, and he says he thinks that Gerrards Cross, being a place of no military importance, surrounded by places that are of military importance, ought to be as safe as anywhere. So, if you wouldn't be too worried, my darlingest Mama, I would rather stay…

I seem to have made rather a hit with a man who gave me a lift as far as Ealing yesterday, as he rang up at lunchtime today & asked me to go for a walk with him. He is a very innocuous young man called Ian, & seems to be quite important in the aircraft industry. He arrived on a motorbike and suggested we should go for a walk in Bulstrode Park, the other end of the village, to which we went on his motorbike, me clinging on for dear life and hoping that the girlish skirt was more adequate than it felt!

He is a very reliable, guileless sort of man – about 25, I suppose – not quite up to Newland standard but quite pleasant. You don't think me rash or anything, do you, because you couldn't imagine anyone less exciting. Well, he showed me a photo of his mother and likes Jeffrey Farnol, so I don't think it will be a life-long friendship, and I really think it's only that he lives with his family in Beaconsfield and thought it would be a more pleasant way of spending a sunny afternoon for us to go for a walk than for him to sit about at home. What I mean is, that I'm not developing into a fast girl, and he is the sort of man with whom one could go for a walk as an acquaintance but not make a life-long friend of. I am discriminative, because another man asked me to have a drink at The French Horn with him and I was most firm and refused. Really, all this explanation is about absolutely nothing, except that Ian is thinking of joining the Home Guard, who apparently give an occasional dance, which he murmured something about, so if I wrote for my dance-frock, if you thought it would be OK (he is too respectable for words) perhaps you could very sweetly send it?... I really don't think I've ever met such an entirely uninteresting young man – you would have laughed at the photo of his mother.

Monday. Your lovely letter just arrived, I am thrilled with the heavenly Coty talc and velouty, how clever of you, and it is sweet of you to amass reserves for me. I do think life without talc or eau-de-c. is rather unthinkable, don't you? ... I love hearing about the nice normal things you are doing at home – I wonder if the snowdrops and things are coming out. The golden crocuses in Hyde Park look so sweet, all round the guns and sandbags...'

Reading those letters to my mother so many years later, I smile at my descriptions of tea with Gwen and my afternoon with the hapless Ian and his passion for the Regency romance novels of Jeffrey Farnol. Though the war had been going on for almost a year and a half, we still retained our sense of humour, and as the letters show, I had the usual teenage preoccupations, but the talk of imminent invasion, which was on everybody's minds, and the mustard gas and the guns and the sandbags in Hyde Park reminds me that 1941 was no ordinary year. London was under attack night after night.

From time to time, I still think of those London mothers putting their children to bed in the stuffy underground station shelters in anticipation of a raid and facing the very real prospect that they might emerge into the daylight next morning to discover that their homes had been destroyed. How scared for those poor children and for themselves they must have been.

CHAPTER SEVEN

Patricia

When I completed my course at the Triangle, the college found me a job as a secretary at Pearn, Pollinger and Higham, a literary agency based just off the Strand in central London. Among their famous clients was the novelist Graham Greene, who had recently published *The Power and The Glory*.

As I could no longer live in the college, I took a room in Berrylands, Surbiton, where I was put on fire watch by night. Fortunately, in all the nights I was on duty, there were no fires to be put out but I confess to being a little disappointed that I never got to raise the alarm by vigorously clashing together two metal dustbin lids as per the instructions in the training manual.

Now that I was a working woman, I travelled into central London before eight every morning because the train was cheaper then. I had become quite left-wing by this time and used to harangue the commuters who travelled in my carriage, pressing copies of *The Worker* upon them and reading aloud long articles about the merits of communist Russia. They were all very good-natured about it, though I'm sure their hearts sank as they saw me board the train each day.

At Pearn, Pollinger and Higham, I assisted all the agency's clients including several American correspondents such as Quentin Reynolds, who had all his papers sent to a suite at The Savoy. I met the crime writer and poet Dorothy L. Sayers. She was an impressively tall woman, who would sit in the office, wreathed in cigarette smoke, interviewing cooks. I also met a number of members of the Sitwell family. The poet Dame Edith was very tall and reminded me of a Tudor portrait of Elizabeth I. Sir Osbert was terribly serious. The art and music critic Sir Sacheverell was my favourite. He was very nice indeed.

As a secretary, I typed up and sent off our writers' short stories to various magazines. If they were returned "rejected" I would give them new covers so that the next recipient wouldn't know they had already been sent out elsewhere and returned. Over lunch-time, I manned the switchboard. It wasn't really a "career" job for me. Though I had considered journalism while at school, I wasn't sure I still wanted to be a writer . I was just filling in time until I could apply to the women's services.

Other people were less keen to sign up for active service. My landlord in Berrylands was determined to sit out the whole war. He had an idea that he could improve his chances of dodging conscription by applying to become a submariner. He certainly didn't *want* to be a submariner. His theory was that his history of respiratory infections would mean there was no chance the Royal Navy would want him to serve the war underwater and thus he would be excused altogether. Alas, the Navy's medical officer passed him as completely fit and his cunning plan backfired in the worst possible way.

The Blitz was still going on, of course, and I heard some awful stories as I travelled into work on the train, including the tale of a German airman brought down over the East End who had been torn limb from limb by angry mothers in revenge for a school that had been hit in a raid. I got used to the sound of the huge anti-aircraft guns in Hyde Park. I also soon became expert, as we all did, at telling the difference between our planes and the Luftwaffe's bombers just by the noise of their engines. The German planes made a sort of staccato "Brrrp Brrrp Brrrp" sound compared to the RAF planes' smoother purr.

One night, the air raid siren sounded while I was up in north London, visiting relations of Edith from Newland Hall. I joined the family in the corrugated iron Anderson Shelter in their back garden, where they kindly made up a bed for me. I remember it was the first time I had ever seen a duvet. I wasn't quite sure what to do with it. Assuming it must work like a sleeping bag, I undid the buttons of the cover and climbed inside. Edith's family must have wondered what I was doing!

Despite the continued danger, I loved being in London. Though the smell of the dust from bombsites hung heavy in the air at all times and you couldn't avoid the devastation that touched every part of the city, there were definitely many moments of levity too. Such as listening to my godmother talk about the moment the Luftwaffe scored a hit on her house in Kensington. As she was stretchered out of the crumbling building, her neighbour took off his hat and held it to his chest in respect, thinking she must be dead. She scared the living daylights out of him by wishing him "good morning".

It was in the September of 1941 that our father was told that his regiment was to be sent overseas at last. The exact location was to be kept strictly under wraps, but my parents devised a code whereby he would be able to tell my mother where he was going. They allocated the names of their friends and neighbours to various countries. Cousin Toby Giles represented India, for example. Kathleen Jenkins the vicar's daughter was a nurse in Singapore, so she came to represent that destination.

We were all together at Newland Hall on the day Daddy left, having spent a lovely week together in Scotland. We waved him off at the train station as he set off on the first leg of his journey, which was back to Lark Hill to join his commanding officer Colonel George Holme and the rest of the regiment. From there, they went to Liverpool to board the ship that would take them to their posting. It was the SS Dominion Monarch, a passenger liner that had been requisitioned for troop transport. They set sail on 29 September.

I wrote in my diary that night. *"Everyone rather remarkably cheerful, thought we might well have been somewhat depressed. It's worst for poor Mama and Bob, of course. Doesn't affect me and Jean greatly. Sometimes wonder if I'm getting rather callous."*

I think perhaps Jean and I were putting a brave face on it. Though we were all immensely proud that our father was off to play his part in the war, we did not know when we would see him again.

After our father's departure, I was at the PPH Agency for only another month or so before I became ill and had to return to Lancashire.

Since Grandboffin kept cows, all through my childhood I'd drunk their milk. It wasn't pasteurised and there was no TT test at the time, so I was always coming down with bovine tuberculosis. Luckily Jean and Bobby somehow managed not to catch it. The symptoms of bovine TB included a dramatic swelling of the glands in my neck. I suffered bouts all through my childhood, right up until I was 21. The only cure for the situation at that time was to have the swollen glands removed: an unpleasant surgical procedure that was usually done under anaesthetic.

So I had to leave PPH and go back to Newland Hall to recuperate. As it happened, the timing was somewhat auspicious. I'd never really settled into my first job, thinking it rather frivolous to be sending out short stories while the country was at war. My colleagues at PPH tried to convince me otherwise, saying that the writers were bringing valuable US dollars into the UK, but from my point of view, it looked as though we were sending rather more money *to* the US than we were getting back. At the same time, wartime rules had come in regarding the use of stationery that filled my day-to-day life with petty tribulations, such as having to cut the agency's labels down to the "correct" dimensions to comply with regulations regarding a parcel label's maximum size. Never mind that the labels had been printed long before the legislation, so the off-cuts were sheer waste. Such frustrations made me itch to join the women's services even more.

CHAPTER EIGHT

Jean

After our father left for his overseas posting, Bobby and I went back to school again. I somehow felt much more isolated now that Daddy was properly away and longed for the post to bring news of him, which, to begin with, it did on a fairly regular basis. Our mother wrote to him every day and he in turn made sure to send letters home every time the SS Dominion Monarch made a stop on its long journey.

Our father's ship was part of a convoy which comprised some twenty liners and cargo boats with an escort of cruisers and destroyers. After leaving the Mersey, the convoy took a wide detour, sailing almost to the coast of North America, before turning south towards Freetown in Sierra Leone on the west coast of Africa. The ship spent two days there, taking on supplies and fresh water for the onward voyage, which offered our father a chance to write and let us know how he was getting on. We weren't surprised to hear that he had been amusing himself and his fellow passengers by putting on nightly entertainments. He had a fine tenor voice and loved to sing. He had even sung with the actress Thora Hird, one of Lancashire's most famous lasses (she would go on to present *Praise Be* and star in *Last of the Summer Wine*). One of my favourite things was to join in as my father led the family in a round of sea shanties of an evening. He told us that onboard ship they called him "the Singing Major".

After Sierra Leone, the SS Dominion Monarch's next stop was Cape Town, South Africa. In Cape Town, the ship and its passengers were welcomed royally for a four-day stay. From there, our father cleverly sent home Christmas presents for the whole family, knowing that the gifts would likely take weeks to get back to Lancashire. From South Africa, our father's voyage continued across the Indian Ocean to Colombo in Sri Lanka, where he had just a few hours on land. And on 29 November he reached Keppel Harbour in Singapore. In a letter to our mother, our father duly asked her to send his regards to Kathleen Jenkins, whose name had come to represent the Malaysian city state in their secret code.

After eight weeks at sea, our father must have longed for a short respite, but he was soon on his way to Kajang, 250 miles north of Singapore near the border with Kuala Lumpur. He didn't have much time to get used to his new environment before he got word that the Japanese had bombed Singapore and landed troops on the north-east coast of Malaya. It was very worrying to hear the bad news from the Far East on the newsreels while I myself felt so far away from home at Wroxall Abbey.

Not long after the Japanese landed in Malaya came the event which truly took the war worldwide. Throughout the conflict so far, the United States had remained mostly on the sidelines, declining to join the fighting though at the same time agreeing to sell the British arms at an exorbitant interest rate. Meanwhile, during the summer of 1941, the Japanese had occupied French Indo-China. That invasion had prompted Britain and the US President Franklin D. Roosevelt to freeze Japanese assets. As a result, the Japanese escalated their aggression, attacking the US Pacific Fleet base at Pearl Harbour in Hawaii on 7 December 1941. The Americans were caught on the hop and lost 15 ships in a matter of hours. The very next day, the US declared war on Japan. Three days later, on 11 December, Hitler declared war on the United States.

With all this going on, Christmas 1941 was necessarily a very different one for the Owtram family of Newland Hall. Never before had Pat, Bobby and I had a Christmas at home without our father at the centre of the celebrations.

In the countryside around us, life went on and there were still parties, of course. Our neighbours the Welches threw one, pulling together a festive meal that Pat described as "*a perfect triumph of ration-evasion and camouflaged ersatz.*" At the Alan Storeys, where we attended a sherry party, Pat took umbrage at one local chap who had an RAF desk job but was strutting about like a decorated fighter pilot.

At home, we had a small Christmas tree, which our mother and Robert had cut for themselves. It didn't seem quite right to have a big one as we usually did. The small tree reflected the subdued mood we were all feeling. As the 25th drew closer we were cheered to receive our father's gifts and postcards from Cape Town. He sent stockings for our mother, Pat and me, which were gratefully received, as they were rationed. We raised a toast to him on the day and hoped he was having a good time wherever he was at that moment.

And then it was time to go back to school again, leaving behind a very sickly Pat, who had contracted pneumonia. The journey to school was quite an adventure. It was snowing hard as I left Lancaster and it wasn't long before my train got stuck. When I didn't turn up at school as expected, the Wroxall Abbey English mistress was despatched to Birmingham to look for me there. Unfortunately by the time my train finally reached Birmingham, she had given up looking for me and gone back to school so that I was on my own again. In the end, my journey of 150 miles took more than 27 hours!

By now, I was beginning to feel as Pat must have done in her last two terms at Wroxall Abbey. School suddenly seemed rather unimportant in the scheme of things. All that mattered was winning the war and getting Daddy back to Newland Hall again safely. The news coming out of Singapore and Malaya was getting worse by the day. A cable arrived at Newland Hall on 17 January, which was some comfort if light on detail. Daddy wrote from Singapore, "VERY FIT, AM ENJOYING REST AFTER RATHER STRENUOUS TIME LATELY, LOVE TO ALL."

At the end of January I wrote home from my boarding house:

Laurels
30/1/42

My own most darling Mummy,

Thank you very much for your letter. I had 2 letters from Daddy! One written on Nov 11th and one on Nov 20th. It is lovely to feel that he was actually writing them, although I didn't know anything about it. He sounded quite happy, though hot! Oh mummy darling! I do so hope you aren't too worried, though I know you can't help being rather. I expect I'm a fatalist or something, but I'm quite certain that he'll be all right, because he's so very precious and God doesn't let anything too awful happen. So I'm certain sure that everything will come out all right in the end. Meanwhile, one can't do anything oneself, so I think one just oughtn't to let oneself get obsessed by the thought of what might happen. Bless you, my most precious Mummy. I wish I was at home with you just now. I'm awfully glad you've got Pat, she's such a help if one's worried. I felt that I must write to you after I heard the one o'clock news, altho' it wasn't bad or anything. Goodnight for now, and more tomorrow.

Sunday. I'm going to ask if I can ring you up tonight or tomorrow so by the time you get this I shall probably have done so. That's just in case you've had any news. I haven't heard it yet today but I'm going to listen in at one. Oh mummy darling! I wish I could be with you until the news gets better again, though I don't know what I could do if I was. Anyway, I'm finding all the religious teaching that I've had is the greatest help. Thank you very, very much for letting me be prepared for confirmation by the Canon. I'm sure no one else could have made God so real that prayers are such a comfort. This all sounds very affected and hypocritical but really I am finding that things are much easier and that I worry much less if I leave them to God instead of trying to look after them myself.

I don't feel that "school news" matters at the moment so I'm not going to put in all about the snow and everything. Only that everyone is very kind and sympathetic and I'm very happy really and, I'm afraid, live very much in the present most of the time. But I don't think it matters being forgetful really. I wish you could be too. My own darlingest mummy, I shall be so thinking of you all the time.

With all my love from
Jinks.

CHAPTER NINE

Patricia

I spent the early months of 1942 at home in Lancashire, recovering from my latest bout of bovine TB and a nasty dose of pneumonia. Though at last I was 18, I was beginning to doubt whether I would *ever* be fit and well enough to join the WAAF. I was also beginning to doubt that I should join the WAAF in any case. Over Christmas, we'd heard from family friends, who had a daughter already in the WAAF, that it wasn't quite what she'd expected and had she known what it was really like, she wouldn't have signed up at all. Apparently the WAAF was getting something of a *reputation*.

While I was briefly away, visiting an old school friend in Wales, my godmother Aunt Ellie wrote to my mother with an alternative suggestion. She said that she knew of a "crowd of jolly girls", Foreign Office secretaries, who were all on their way to do war work at a large house in Buckinghamshire. Perhaps I would like to join them rather than one of the women's forces? When Mummy relayed the message, I thought it sounded like the dreariest kind of war work imaginable and I responded hastily and briefly by telegram, starting, "Hate crowds jolly girls". The man in the telegraph office who took my message told me, "I hate crowds of jolly girls too." Many years later, I would find out that the big house full of jolly girls had in fact been Bletchley Park.

Instead, I looked to my mother's brother Charles Saumarez Daniel, Uncle Tid, captain of the destroyer HMS Faulknor, to persuade my mother that I should be allowed to try for the Women's Royal Naval Service. My mother's mother, Agnes Saumarez, came from the Channel Islands and it was a well-established tradition that Saumarez men joined the Royal Navy. Why shouldn't that be true of the women as well? Uncle Tid agreed with me. He thought it would be more than appropriate for me to join the WRNS, known as the Wrens for short. I wrote to ask my father if he would approve but I wasn't able to find out what he thought of the idea because in February 1942, there was very bad news indeed.

Since the beginning of December 1941, the Japanese forces had been steadily fighting their way down the Malayan Peninsula, taking 50,000 Allied troops prisoner as they did so. In February 1942, they made it to Singapore, the most important British military base in South East Asia. The Japanese were a formidable enemy. Their tanks and their air superiority gave them a huge advantage over the Allied troops in the area who had hardly any air cover at all.

Having been in the north of the peninsula, our father was back in Singapore as the worst of the horror unfolded. We knew that much because he had managed to send a cable on 7 February. Around that time, I was writing him a letter (which I completed over several days), having learned elsewhere that members of the 137th Regiment, including Colonel George Holme, had been declared missing.

Newland Hall,
Near Lancaster
8th February, 1942

My darling Daddy,
We have heard such a lot about the Regiment this week, mostly through Mrs Holme. I was very sorry to hear from her that her husband, Major Spencer, and Lieut. Moss are among the missing, and also to see Finlay Mangall's name in The Times *as missing: I've cut out all the cuttings I have seen, and we keep all the news from Malaya for your cutting-book. It's so wonderful that you got back to Singapore safely, and I'm sure you must have had a very "strenuous" time indeed. I am*

afraid it will be far from peaceful for you at the moment, too, and I wonder very much where in Singapore you are (I know the geography of it very well now).

It is of course the news-highlight at present, and sometimes there are very good accounts of life there on the wireless. It must be a most extraordinary experience, and very interesting after it's all over. But I do wish it was all over and that you were safely at home again. One can hardly believe that you are there in the middle of it, specially as life goes on so normally here. Every time I write I wonder so much where you will be when you read it, and how the position will have changed!

Monday. This seems to be devolving into a serial letter, as it is Monday evening and so I will probably have to finish it tomorrow. The news from Singapore is rather disquieting, as the Japs have got a bridgehead on the NW coast. Darling Daddy, you are so much in our thoughts just now and I do so hope you are not right at the front, though Singapore seems so small that it must be mostly front. I'd no idea the Johore Strait was anything like so narrow and shallow as we're told now it is. We will all be so glad when the present phase is over and when we have some news of you!

The snowdrops are just beginning to come out here, very small, short ones, but they smell so lovely and fresh and like spring. Soon there will be violets and Lent Lilies too. I found masses and masses of snowdrop buds in the little wood at the end of the garden today.

Tuesday. Your cable of Feb 7th (last Saturday) has just come, and we're all so glad to have it. How clever of you to get it out in time, we're letting everyone know – I wrote to Bob and am ringing Jean up, and I can't tell you how delighted we are. It was so very sweet and thoughtful of you, and I'm so glad some of our letters (even though five months old!) have arrived. People ring up every day to ask if we have news of you, and it's lovely to have something so recent to tell them. People are so kind, and the most casual acquaintances ring us up or write.

The news from Singapore today is that there's been another Jap landing, and the situation is awfully serious. Oh darling Daddy, it's so awful waiting for news. Your cable was such a comfort, really a link, and I do hope perhaps you have a staff job or something else important and aren't all among the dive-bombers etc. Anyway, I know you will be splendid whatever you're doing, and we're all so proud of you, but we do wish it was all over and we could put the rods in the back of the car and set off for Arisaig! This letter must stop now.

Your admiring Trish.

There was bad news closer to home as well. On Friday 13 February, I wrote in my diary of the German navy's latest daring move, as they repositioned some of their most feared battle-ships. The Scharnhorst and The Gneisenau were infamous.

The Scharnhorst sank the auxiliary cruiser HMS Rawalpindi in 1939 and together with The Gneisenau, it was responsible for the sinking of the aircraft carrier HMS Glorious and Acasta and Ardent, the destroyers in HMS Glorious' escort, in June 1940. That these German cruisers were still at large was a cause of great anguish.

> *"Scharnhorst, Gneisenau and Prinz Eugen slipped out of Brest and up the Channel under perfect weather conditions yesterday. Our swordfish aircraft attacked them, also other aircraft and naval vessels, but we lost 42 aircraft and didn't get the ships. They were never expected to go up the Channel, and our dispositions were all made in the Atlantic. Grand furore about this, but to no purpose now. S, G and PE now safely in the Heligoland Bight. Our forces were splendid but they had all the luck plus a huge fighter-umbrella. As they passed up the French coast flights of fighters relieved each other. Bad visibility discounted our coastal guns. I suppose some day our luck will turn: we could certainly do with a spot more."*

That change in luck didn't come quickly enough for my father's regiment. On 15 February, Singapore fell. The Japanese forced the British to surrender the island-state and some 80,000 further men, women and children were made prisoners of war. It was the largest ever surrender of British led forces, leading Churchill to declare it the "worst disaster" in British military history.

I was at home with Mummy and Grandboffin when it happened. Mummy was quite unwell at the time and Grandboffin and I had been doing our best to shelter her from the worst. Unfortunately, when the doctor came to visit, he told her everything.

We were all stunned by the news, made worse by the fact that for the time being, we had no idea whatsoever whether my father was among those POWs or whether he had been injured or even died in the fighting. Since his cable on 7 February, sent out before the surrender, we'd heard nothing. All we could do was wait and pray and try not to think about the horrifying stories about Japanese prisoner of war camps and the atrocities perpetrated within them that filled the daily newsreels and papers.

My mother kept herself distracted with running the house and with her ARP work, which had to go on, of course. She was a very strong-minded woman though I could see she was under great strain. We were helped too, by the support of the wider family and friends. We received more than 30 letters in the week after the news broke. But it was not easy to stay optimistic.

On 24 February, we heard that Kathleen Jenkins, the vicar's daughter, had stayed on in Singapore to support the

British troops in her role as nurse rather than be evacuated. How brave she was. Then on 8 March, our mother received a letter from the War Office regarding our father, telling her, "Every endeavour is being made through diplomatic and other channels to obtain information concerning him, and it is hoped that he is safe although he may be a Prisoner of War. It will be necessary, however, to post him as "Missing" pending receipt of some definite information."

A notice was duly posted in the West Lancashire Gazette later that month. The cutting, which I glued into my diary, contained excerpts from a letter my father sent home on 17 January, in which he had elaborated on his Regiment's retreat to Singapore. They'd been bombed on land and in a train and even had to swim a river. He wrote of his injured colleagues, "They are all doing well and in wonderful spirits and every one of them has only one thought – to get back to the Regiment and have another crack at the Japs." How poignant it was to read such optimism knowing what had happened a couple of weeks later.

On 16 March George Holme's wife called to say that she too had received a letter from our father, posted before Singapore fell. It contained the very worst news for her and her family. My diary entry reads, *"Mrs Holme rang up to say she had just heard from Daddy, account of George Holme's death. GH insisted on going off alone on motorbike to see what had happened to ½ the Regt. who were cut off – was killed by Jap tank. Letter dated Jan 20 from D, enclosing photo. He lost all his belongings in Malaya, regt had heavy casualties, D had miraculous escape."*

Weeks later, the letter I'd sent to my father on 8 February would be returned stamped "Addressee reported missing."

CHAPTER TEN

Patricia

Not knowing my poor father's fate made me all the more determined to sign up as soon as I could. I couldn't sit by and do nothing. As I'd said in another letter to Daddy, which was also returned with that dreaded "addressee reported missing" stamp, "*I foresee people asking me as long as I live what I did in the war, and it won't be much fun to be one of the few who didn't do anything.*"

Having decided against the WAAF, I'd written to the Wrens back in January, applying for a position as a Signals Distributing Office Watchkeeper (whatever that was, as I said in my diary of the time) or something in Communications, but it seemed to be taking an age for them to get back to me. At last, in March, I was invited for a medical. I was passed, except that my latest bout of Bovine TB was still evident as a swollen gland in my neck. For that reason my call-up was deferred pending a further examination in a few weeks' time.

I used that time to brush up my German, which Uncle Tid had assured me would be very useful. I spent most evenings in the maid's parlour with Lilly, who had become a good friend. We often travelled into Lancaster together to shop or to watch films. She introduced me to the work of a number of French directors she admired.

At the end of April, my mother's father, Colonel Charles Daniel, known to us as "Pops", was evacuated to Newland Hall after he was bombed out of the hotel in Bath where he had been living when the city was hit by one of the Germans' so-called "Baedeker Raids". Unlike towns such as Portsmouth and Coventry, which were blitzed because they were home to military bases or factories, the targets of the Baedeker raids were chosen for their cultural significance. They included Canterbury, Norwich, York and Exeter. Bath was targeted for its beautiful 18th-century architecture. The city's elegant Assembly Rooms were destroyed, as were houses in the famous Royal Crescent and Circus. 417 people were killed.

We continued to wait for news of my father but once again I tried to shield my mother from the worst reports coming out of the Far East. I wrote in my diary on 12 May, *"Am terrified that atrocity stories will leak out from Singapore and perturb M. There can never have been such a deadly outburst of worldwide cruelty as now…"*

The death toll was rising on all sides. On 31 May, the RAF bombed Cologne. I longed to hear good news from France. All these things I recorded in my diary while it seemed I would never get to play my part. Then, finally, on Friday 24 July, I was summoned to Liverpool for my WRNS German test.

The test took place in a room – the Admirals' Conference Room, as it happened – in the city's famous Liver Building. As I walked in, my eyes were immediately drawn to a baize covered table upon which lay a machine gun. A young naval officer was supervising my test. When he saw me staring at the gun, he told me, "Nobody's supposed to see that." Apparently, it was the newest technology. I didn't let on that it meant nothing much to me. He was obviously very proud of it.

When I got home, I recalled the day's events. *"Rather melodramatic, incredible and historic day… Test 30" oral (v. satisfactory) and 3 hrs written (not so). Had hasty lunch at 12.45 and just was able to leave Admirals' Conference Room before ingress of Admirals. On leaving Lieut. G, went to WRNS recruiting office in Old Hall St, and future suddenly became rather staggering, owing to me having passed test. Am filled with astonishment, pride and feeling of crushing responsibility!*

"… feel that this is probably the high-light of my life. If it is, I am glad it's come while I am still young enough to enjoy it. Very few people of my age (19 and a month) do, after all, get a break like this. I feel almost that it's too good to be true!"

I was going to be a Wren!

I was finally called up in August 1942, in the middle of a tremendous heatwave. I was sent a railway warrant to take me from Lancashire to Mill Hill, just outside London, where I would spend two weeks in "general training". It took a little while to get used to it. Though my training took place entirely on dry land, everything at the WRNS base was referred to in naval terms. The building had been given the name HMS Pembroke III, as if it were a ship. Floors were decks. Our dormitories, where we slept in double bunks, were cabins. The kitchen was a galley. Tea-breaks were taken at the "tea-boat". We had to learn KR (King's Regulations) and AI (Admiralty Instructions). We were taught how to march and how to salute.

There was a lot to learn. Not only with regard to the naval routine and the daily drills. Up until now, I'd lived a somewhat sheltered existence. The Triangle College and Pearn, Pollinger and Higham had been full of people from the social circles in which I'd grown up. For the first time, I would be living and working alongside people from all walks of life. On my first day in Mill Hill, I learned that one of my fellow new recruits, who came from the East End, had been what my parents' generation might have called a "tart". I was a little shocked when she told me about her previous employment but was pleased to discover that she was very nice indeed. It made me feel rather grown up to be training alongside her as an equal.

Soon after I arrived at the training camp, I wrote to my mother.

WRNS Training Depot,
Ridgeway,
Mill Hill
NW7
Thursday

My own darling Mum,

... I must tell you a bit about this place.

It is a vast building, started as a cancer research centre and then left empty for 2 years, until the Admiralty recently took it over. Mill Hill seems to be miles out of London, about halfway to York, and all fields and woods with a few houses. One really feels absolutely cut off from everywhere! It is all concrete, and only about half built – at least, it is all over scaffolding etc. There is no furniture at all except long deal tables with chairs in the mess-deck and two-tier bunks and little chests of drawers in the cabins. I am writing this in my bunk, I managed to grab a top one; my watch doesn't have to appear till eight o'clock breakfast, which doesn't seem too strenuous! I think the food seems good and I slept like a log in my comfy bunk – but I was very glad of the pillow. I had a lovely hot bath – you can have one whenever you like, and the water is boiling. We have nice sheets and blankets issued to us, which will be changed on Monday.

This is the biggest Wren training Depot – my own new entry is about 400. They are all quite pleasant, one or two are "our own sort", including a very nice girl called Burnett-Stewart from Pitlochry, but unfortunately she is in a different division and cabin, so I don't have much chance of seeing her.

At 8.30 we have a squad drill on the roof, and the rest of the day we spend at lectures, I think. All the staff are very nice indeed and couldn't be more helpful. But my, it is an ugly uniform! Everywhere is nicely labelled, SICK BAY and CAPTAIN'S OFFICE, and on each floor there is a main deck (which is a long passage) and subsidiary decks off at each corner.

I think I like it OK, for a short time anyway. But one feels a bit swamped by such a mass of people at first!

P.S. I've remembered several other things, so here is some more! I hope my telegram arrived – darling the sandwiches were delicious. The journey was very good, my carriage was never full, and when we arrived I went along to Selfridges and got a pretty red (couldn't get cherry colour) sash and flower for my frock. It was so sweet of you to alter the petticoat so beautifully. I am longing to wear it.

I wonder if you could be an angel and type on an envelope for me to send to Daddy? It must have been a thrilling raid on Dieppe, judging from the headlines – when I saw BRITISH FORCES AND TANKS LAND IN FRANCE – HEAVY

FIGHTING – I thought "Whoopee, the second front!" But no. But I shouldn't think it will be long now.

Well my darlingest, I must stop. I am thinking of you so much, I do miss you so. But I'm sure I will be happy here, so don't worry.

I don't know who I was trying to convince that everything would be all right in that particular letter. Mummy or myself! Though we were all putting a brave face on it, of course we were still very worried about my father and I felt that it was easier to deal with that worry when we were all together somehow.

At least, by now, we knew that Daddy had survived the Fall of Singapore. His name appeared on the list of prisoners of war that the Japanese had released via the Red Cross. But though that was some comfort, we knew that by the time the message reached us, it was old news and meant only that he had been alive when the list was taken. There was no detailed information and we'd heard nothing since.

A little later, I wrote to Mummy again and amongst other things, I asked if she was really, really sure that I shouldn't come home when my training ended. After that, it would be much more difficult.

HMS Pembroke III
c/o GPO London
Thursday (11.50)

(*I cheer up later on!)

My own darling Mum,

*Another line while I wait for a lecture… I am furious to see that it is the most heavenly day of the summer so far. It would have to choose the time when I'm encloistered in concrete! We did do a bit of squad drill outside which was lovely.

We have been issued with navy overalls and look even more like a women's reformatory than ever. I am glad I am only here for two weeks because I think that will be quite enough. It will be much nicer to be on a job. We have prayers each morning you will be pleased to hear. It is called Divisions… Oh darling darling, what a time it does seem since I left you! The first day or two are always the longest, aren't they?

(Friday morning) I think when I get settled down a bit I'll like this place all right. I feel very fit and the food is quite good, and all the staff and most of the girls are very friendly. We have a charming padre, a retired naval chaplain, who gave us a really beautiful talk yesterday on 'The Spirit of the Service'. He also said that any rating can go straight to a chaplain without having to do it through the Petty Officer, as is necessary if you wish to approach any other officer. I do

wish these two weeks were over and I was drafted somewhere. They expect you to loathe it to start with, and we all do. But one does find that it has more and more compensations: it's lovely to get a hot bath night and morning and there's a very good canteen. I'm not unhappy darling, but I do miss you and everyone and everything at home and it's awful to think it's only two days since I left, because what it feels like is 100 years!

Our pay to start with is ¼ and 4d war bonus a day, which is 10/8 a week and 2/8 kit upkeep allowance = the glorious sum of 13/4 a week! Of course it does rise with you. They pay you fortnightly – to the nearest 2/- below, and keep the balance as a credit due to you in the ship's ledger, also as a security for them in case you desert with some admiralty property! It is paid back again quarterly.

I'm longing to get my uniform and depart to a port. We don't have to swear an oath of allegiance because the King takes our loyalty for granted! He has a nerve, hasn't he, after he did you-know-what about those hats.

I suppose I oughtn't to describe my ship to you, except to say that its size is staggering, and there are hundreds of workmen all over it always. The local village is quite useless, bleak and waste-papery.

I do adore being with you so much, darlingest, and it seems a waste of time not being. 21 days a year won't be nearly enough – but let's hope the war will hurry up and be over. I don't think I'll ever regret the Wrens. In fact I'm sure I will love it. But I wish I was

at a nice friendly little depot instead of this vast and bleak one!
However, a fortnight doesn't last long, and it will just have to be got
through. The girls are mostly a nice type – some are very nice.

(Friday 14:10 hrs) This started as a rather dejected letter,
I fear, but I am feeling quite quite different now, in fact I really
am enjoying it. The first day and most of yesterday were awful,
and this morning was rather drear, but I seem to have got used to
it suddenly, and what with that and the weekend coming, I feel
another woman (I mean, another rating). I adore squad-drill,
we have 2 drills a day – well, here is a typical day's programme:

08.00	*breakfast*
08.30	*squad drill on the roof*
08.45	*divisions*
09.30	*squad drill on the road*
10.00	*day's orders and notices*
10.30	*tea boat*
11.00	*lectures, till*
13.00	*dinner*
14.00	*interviews or lecture*
14.30	*lecture*
15.30	*tea boat*
16.00	*games or PT*
17.00	*lectures till*
19.00	*supper*

After which one is free till lights out at 21.30. There never seems to be a free moment during the day, but it is all very well organised and the lectures are fascinating. Thank heavens you never salute under a roof, as life would be impossible with an officer every other yard. I do love all this really, darling, though no doubt I shall continue to grumble about it as I do now.

(Saturday morning early) I think this must be the wrong time of day for me to write to you, because I do miss you so terribly much in the mornings – indeed, all day I do, but it is worst now with nothing to distract one. Oh darling, how could I leave you! I do love you so much, my darling Mama; tell me, would it make all the difference in the world to you (said she slightly conceitedly) if I was at home next winter? If it would, darling, angel, I can leave at the end of the fortnight and come. Oh, if only I'd thought about it a bit more instead of panting so much to go! I'm not just saying this because I don't like this place – it isn't that, because anyway I do like it. But it seems so irrevocable to sign a form at the end of these two weeks which means that I just won't be able to see you ever for more than three weeks in the year. Oh my darling, you must think I am as weak as water, vacillating about like this. It's just that I realise now how much more important it is that you should be happy than that I should spend the war in an unbecoming blue hat. There are I know war jobs near home, and I will be content if you feel you'd like me to come. It wouldn't be "a waste of my

time" if I was doing war work. But don't think darling that it's because I loathe the WRNS. I like the camaraderie and the naval background and all that most immensely.

(10.15 hours) Do disregard the mournful wails I emit in the doleful dawn. We are now awaiting a lecture and I feel full of cheer and tea-boat. This morning I had a talk to a rather nice girl called Oosterveen (Dutch?) who is going on the same job as me. We are about seven altogether, I think, and we go for a week's trial to a quite civilised place (don't pass any of all this on) not far from where I was in digs, then if we pass I believe we leave the course-station automatically as Petty Officers, which will be marvellous. They wear brass buttons with anchors on them, and tricorne hats with naval badges, and crossed anchors on the sleeve, and are saluted by all the lesser fry and command great respect (plus good pay) and to any outsider look just like Wren officers. Isn't it a thrill? Darling, if it only comes off! Of course it WON'T – I shan't come through the course, or they'll say I'm too young to be a PO – oh, endless possibilities! Would you be proud to have a Petty Officer for a daughter?

After the course we would all be sent to a large house on the S. or E. coast where we would live in solitary splendour outwitting Gross-Admiral Raeder! But it's much more likely that I shall fail, and be sent back here to remuster as a steward or typist. Darling, there were two copies of "Die Zeitung", the free-German newspaper, in my room – could I please have those

78

if they haven't gone to salvage. Could you please get me any copies, ancient or modern, of it in Lanc. I am forgetting all my German and I DO want to pass this week.

We have just had an ARP lecture. Gosh, how terrifying these brand new HE incendiaries are! Heaven preserve us from phosphorous burns.

(Saturday evening, 19.45 hours) I have found a really charming girl who is going on the same job as me, we spent this evening at the Toc H together. She is most delightful, pretty and de notre cercle and widely travelled and hasn't done any German since the war, so is about as nervous as I am. We are going to talk it together in the evenings. We both passionately want those tricorne hats! Oh darling, I never thought to aspire to one of those!!! They are so becoming...

Bye bye for now my darlingest – I am quite happy now I've found what nice people I shall be with, and what fun the job will be. I went to the early and the second service today. Oh please darling, could you get me the adorable hat?

Oceans of love,
From Pat.

CHAPTER ELEVEN

Patricia

Despite my homesick letters from Mill Hill, I did not throw in the towel and go home at the end of those two weeks' basic training. My mother convinced me that she and Grandboffin could spare me. I'd also heard that I was going to be drafted to a very interesting position, which reassured me that it wouldn't be all marching and saluting for evermore.

Thanks to my proficiency in German, I'd been chosen to go to a house in Southmead, in south-west London, to train as a special duties linguist, alongside a few other Mill Hill girls that I'd grown to like in our fortnight together. Things were looking up, as I told my mother in this letter, sent home on my first day on the new course.

Chapter Eleven

30. VIII. 42

WRNS Depot
Rosedale
Victoria Drive,
Wimbledon, SW19

My own darling Mum,

Well, here we are, and we aren't quite sure that it isn't heaven by some mistake, or else that we'll wake up back at M.H. Oh boy, this is the most incredibly lovely place – honestly darling, it's like the Ritz after that concrete skyscraper.

We left at 2.15 today, our luggage went in a van and we seven set sail in a bus. It was a celestial moment, handing in our station cards at Regulating for the last time, and buzzing off ashore. We had a large tea at Cole's in Baker Street, and finally arrived here about 5.30. There are only ten people here altogether, we sleep in a delightful house, eat in another, and work in yet another. The staff are charming and it's so marvellous to live in a civilised house and have saucers with our cups – we are all full of joie-de-vivre.

– and now for a week of ghastly strain. I don't really feel very optimistic about it, darling, I'm afraid, specially as I know what we do now. Tomorrow I sign the Official Secrets Act (!) and I won't be able to tell you anything ever, so you will try to forget all about it, won't you darling?

By the way, those that come through do emerge as Acting Petty Officers with tricorn hats! But I fear it won't be me.

I shall be here until Saturday anyway – unless I have a nervous breakdown first, which I believe has happened to some of my predecessors.

Don't tell Daddy where I am, will you: I have to write to him as from home… Probably later on my letters will be censored, so prenez garde.

Oh darling, we're having such a heavenly time. I am enjoying it all so much. Darling, I am so TERRIFICALLY glad I joined the Wrens, all is couleur de rose.

This letter will have to end now as I must post it, and we have long long hours and very little time off. Oh darling, life can be so thrilling. I never knew it could. Not so thrilling. Possibly, I might get a 48 hours the weekend after next. Oh boy, how wizard!

No more, I don't think I was ever so thrilled.

Bye bye my darling – love from Pat.

Signing the Official Secrets Act was a daunting moment for me. As I hovered the tip of my pen over the paper, ready to add my signature, I considered the ramifications. Once I signed, that was it. I really would be able to tell *no-one* – not even my family – what I was going to be doing from then on.

Though I could tell them where I was, I would not be able to breathe a word about my work. We were warned that there was no release from the Act and if we breached it in any way the penalties were harsh indeed. Up to and including death!

It all sounded so serious and hush-hush in a way I'd only ever before seen in films that as I finally scribbled my name at the bottom of the sheet, I worried for a moment that I had just accidentally signed up to be a spy. I pictured myself being parachuted into a distant forest with a fake passport and having to infiltrate the German ranks. In the event, I soon learned that my future role would be a little less dramatic than that, though no less important. I was to become an interceptor with the "Y" service.

"Y" Service operatives worked out of "Y" Stations, where they listened in to enemy radio transmissions. The "Y" actually stood phonetically for "WI" which in turn stood for "Wireless Intercept". Y Stations were operated by all the British forces – the Army, the Navy and The RAF – but also by the Foreign Office and even by the Post Office. All the wireless operators had to sign the Official Secrets Act, as I did, though not all of them were military personnel. More than a 1,000 civilians, self-proclaimed "radio hams", were also recruited to the Radio Security Service by MI5 for their expertise in tracking radio signals and deciphering Morse Code.

As a Wren, I would be listening to signals from the Kriegsmarine, the German navy. The specialist WRNS Y Service course at the Royal Naval Training Establishment Southmead near Wimbledon lasted for two weeks. My fellow course mates and I were under the auspices of Lieutenant L.A. Marshall, known to everyone as Freddie.

Freddie Marshall was in his late twenties by the time I met him. He'd grown up in Denmark and was completely fluent in English, Danish and German. He'd joined the Royal Navy to be a sailor but soon realised that if we were going to prevent a German invasion, intelligence was key. It was essential to be able to listen to German ships as a means of anticipating their movements. Since the Royal Navy's men were mostly required on the front line, Freddie persuaded the WRNS to let him train a specialist team of their young women for the job.

First things first, we were taught yet more British naval terms. Though we had spent two weeks on "HMS Pembroke III" most of us still had no idea whatsoever what went on onboard a real ship. Once we understood those naval terms, we then had to learn their German equivalents. We also had to learn the German phonetic alphabet, which began "A for Anton, B for Bertha etc".

Once we were up to speed with those essentials, Freddie honed our listening skills by reading out messages in German that were broadcast from one room to another over an internal radio system. Our job was to note them down as accurately as we could, armed only with pencils and notepads. Gradually, the messages became more complicated and at the same time Freddie increased their speed and the amount of interference that came with them. At times it could be very frustrating, trying to separate the message from the white noise. I wondered how on earth we were supposed to get it right under real conditions, when every syllable mattered.

Freddie was looking for Wrens with the right kind of temperament as well as good hearing, listening and language skills. We were warned that interceptor work comprised long periods of crushing boredom when nothing happened at all, punctuated by short stints of incredible intensity. Not everyone would be able to cope with the highs and lows. Especially the lows.

It was at Southmead that I learned how to operate an HRO, a large square high-frequency radio receiver, made in America. HRO was rumoured to stand for "Helluva Rush Order", which was an insider joke from the factory where overtime slips were sometimes marked "Hell of a Rush". The HRO looked like a fairly basic instrument with a big dial at its centre, but it was the ultimate in radio technology of the time.

To begin with, one just had to keep slowly turning the dial at the centre of the HRO back and forth until you came across a signal. We were taught the frequencies where we were most likely to find German naval traffic. Once you found a signal, you could use smaller dials to increase the volume or try to clear interference.

When a signal came through, we had to note down on a naval message pad – a foolscap pad divided into squares – first the signal's frequency and then everything we heard. If a message was in code, then each group of four letters had a square to itself. Freddie had designed note pads with a special layout for maximum clarity.

Freddie himself was so very kind and cheering and inspiring. His dedication to turning us new Wrens into effective interceptors made us all the more determined to succeed. As did the promise of a more fetching uniform, at least in my case.

The requisitioned house in Southmead where we Wrens worked and lived really was the height of luxury compared to the dorms we'd lived in for our basic training. We were able to have four hot baths a week. To have so much hot water was quite a treat. Also Mill Hill had seemed in the middle of nowhere so we made the most of being much closer to central London now. Our curfew was eleven o'clock but some of our number would stay out later, meeting boyfriends and the like. We always made sure that the window to the bathroom was left open at night, so that they could climb back in undetected and our senior officers would be none the wiser about their adventures.

That said, my new friend Alison Squire was once caught arriving back at the house at a shocking two minutes past eleven. The following day, at her ticking off, the officer in charge said, "This is not the sort of behaviour we would expect from someone who was once a nun."

"A nun?" Alison was confused.

"Yes, a nun. You wrote in your application that you had been a nun."

"*None!*" said Alison. "Under previous occupation, I wrote *none.*"

I never had to climb through that window myself. My social life was quite sedate but we had an aunt in London – Aunt Marjorie – who was on a committee which put on dances at the Grosvenor House Hotel on Park Lane for visiting American servicemen. She called it The Sunday Club. Left-wing as I was at the time, I didn't particularly want to go along to those dances, but I was expected to do my family duty and help Aunt Marjorie put on a good show. I remember the first time I went along. The dance was being held in the hotel's basement, to avoid any interruption by German bombers, and I was shocked to see that a gallery alongside the makeshift ballroom was lined with beds. What on earth had I signed up for? Of course, the beds were there for the hotel staff to sleep in during air raids.

At the beginning of each dance, Aunt Marjorie would light a candle and cut a cake. I'm not sure quite what the ritual was supposed to symbolise but she did it without fail.

The American charitable organisation with which my aunt worked would send over lots of clothes, which were intended for the people who had lost everything in the Blitz. The gifts were well-intentioned but not always entirely suitable. There were usually lots of unfashionable evening dresses in the bundles. New clothes were rationed, of course. You had to really think about whether you really needed something. We were all having to learn to make do and mend.

At the end of the course in Southmead, I was thrilled when I passed all the tests. After just a few weeks with Freddie, I understood how important the work of the Y Service was and I couldn't wait to do my bit. Upon graduating from the course, I was immediately given the rank of Acting Petty Officer Special Duties (Linguist) Y. We were known colloquially as "Freddie's Fairies".

To go with my new title, I would receive a new uniform, with bright brass buttons and a smart tricorn hat to replace the plain black buttons and round hat which lower rankings wore. The hat was very important to me, adding a dash of panache. I'd been very disappointed when the king himself vetoed the roll-out of attractive new hats for the lower rankings so I was thrilled to be able to swap my round hat for that tricorn. I wrote home to let my mother know that I'd earned the hat I prayed for at last.

From A/PO Owtram
Rosedale
Victoria Drive,
Wimbledon SW19

Saturday 0645 (am)

My own darling Mum,
  Oh darling, isn't it marvellous –
  The Owtram Brain
  Has done it again
  All is well. J'ai passé. It is quite incredible, darling – I mean I never thought I had a chance because the standard is so high. They told us at 10.30 last night, 8 out of 10 got through. It is rather awkward. We feel we can't sing for joy as we would like because of them. But they'll be going back to the Training Depot this morning, poor dears, which will eliminate the embarrassment.
  Immediately after breakfast today (I am still in bunk) we eight proceed by bus to Westfield (which is one of the training depots) in Hampstead, and are approved and photographed. We

shall get our gilt buttons (you have to buy those yourself, it comes to about 10/-) and our crossed killicks (worn on the sleeve) but we may not get our tricorns because they often aren't in stock and have to be ordered. I do hope we will get them soon.

"A/PO" is my correct designation. With any luck it will be confirmed after a few months, then I shall be just "P/O". We probably shan't get a 48 hours after all, as we're very urgently needed. Which means that we shall probably be drafted today or tomorrow week, till when we shall be here.

Oh darling, it is so simply marvellous, the future is one long thrill, if only I hadn't signed the O.S. Act I could tell you, but as I have I can't, nor ever will I be able to, because it also binds you after you leave the service. But darling, everything is so heavenly. Midge passed too, and all the ones I like. Won't it be grand having 35/- a week instead of 13/-! Oh boy oh boy!

...I will try to write to everyone, but this course is very exhaustive. F'rinstance, on our return (in an Admiralty van!) from the kitting establishment, we have to settle down to an afternoon's concentrated activity: on a Saturday! Bye bye darling, from your adoring A/PO. Pat

A day later, we new Acting Petty Officers were kitted out. We went to the training depot where we each collected two navy coats and skirts, a topcoat, two overalls, two pairs of shoes, a respirator and the usual complement of shirts, collars, ties and stockings. Oh, and THE HAT about which I had been so excited. Once suitably dressed, we were taken to a photographer for official photographs though for some reason, they were not taken. Then we piled onto the bus again to get back to Southmead. We arrived in time for lunch but just as we were sitting down, the siren announced an air raid and everyone streamed down into the shelters. Except for three of us who carried on eating, assuming it was just a practice. For once, it wasn't. Finally an air-raid warden came to fetch us, but just as that happened, the all-clear was sounded, which was lucky.

That evening, my friend Midge and I went up to central London for dinner at the Café Royal, proudly wearing our new uniforms. We were treated like duchesses by the restaurant staff and even got salutes from some ATS (Auxiliary Territorial Service) girls.

I couldn't wait to make my own first proper salute. I was determined to make sure that the recipient was worthy of the honour, so together with Alison Squire – who had never been a nun! – I went to St James' Park, where we lay in wait for a suitable target. While we were on the bridge crossing the lake, we saw a likely fellow. He was a very attractive and distinguished-looking naval officer. Pulling ourselves up straight, Alison and I gave him our very smartest salute.

He looked somewhat startled but of course he straight away saluted in return. That was the point at which Alison and I burst into fits of giggles and had to run away. It was such a thrill. I couldn't wait for my first posting.

CHAPTER TWELVE

Jean

1942

I was at school when reports reached Britain of the Fall of Singapore. I understood at once the implications for our family. According to his last cable, our father was right there in the thick of it. What had happened to him? It was simply terrible not to know. I did my best to bear the news stoically. After all, until we had confirmation otherwise, for all I knew Daddy could be alive and well. But it wasn't long before I gave in to unhelpful thoughts of the worst-case scenario and I burst into tears.

The older girls and the teachers of Wroxall Abbey were very kind when they heard what was going on. They did their best to comfort me but away from all my family I suddenly felt very isolated indeed. I can only imagine how it must have been for Bobby, who was also away at school at the time but so much younger. Bobby and I had always been very close and I wished that we might have been together so that we could comfort each other.

The six months it took for the Japanese to release their prisoner of war list felt like years. When I learned that my father's name was on that list, I was relieved of course, but still deeply shaken. My father, a prisoner of war! I couldn't believe it. I had always regarded the great Major Cary Owtram as invincible. I had never imagined it possible that he could end up as anyone's *prisoner*. I was appalled by the idea.

Though I loved school, the events of 1942 made me eager to grow up quickly. As a teenager, I felt so helpless. I was too young to do anything really useful. Pat was off training with the Wrens at last, so she was doing her bit. But I would be leaving school myself soon and I began to wonder how I might play my part. I was itching to be old enough to join the women's services just like my big sister.

I was rising 17 when I left Wroxall Abbey at last. I left without many qualifications and I still couldn't sign up. For that I would need to be 18. So I spent much of my 17th year back at Newland Hall, helping Grandboffin again. His pedigree herd still needed cataloguing. The country shows still went on and he still wanted to show off the cows. Mama still made her nightly rounds as ARP warden, checking the village for any violation of the blackout rules. She still inevitably found that the only stray lights she saw on her rounds blazed from the windows of Newland Hall.

I'm sure I was absolutely intolerable for the period I found myself back at home after leaving school. I resented not having a uniform. Who was I? I felt like a spare part and really hated having to fill in time. At least when Bob was home, he was allowed to practise shooting with Grandboffin.

To keep me out of trouble, it was decided that I should follow Pat's example and go to the Triangle Secretarial College to study office skills and Spanish. I was not an eager student of shorthand or typing but I was glad to be away from home and closer to the action at last. When I went into central London, I was thrilled to see uniformed servicemen and women from all the Allied Nations and dreamed that one day I would join their ranks and earn their respect just as they had mine.

I had hoped that I might follow Pat into the Wrens but by the time I was old enough, the Wrens were only recruiting stewards and cooks and the last thing I wanted was to spend the war in the kitchen or waiting tables! That would be even worse than secretarial college. But what could I do instead?

It was my godmother Aunt Marjorie who first drew my attention to the First Aid Nursing Yeomanry – the FANY as it was known. I had no idea at the time what it was that the

FANY did but Aunt Marjorie said that the FANY recruits seemed to be having a "very good time" in London.

I soon learned that the FANY was a voluntary organisation, founded in 1907 after the Boer War, to support both civilian and military operations in times of emergency. For those early recruits, being able to ride a horse was a must. During the First World War, the FANY had provided a valuable ambulance service, bringing injured men and women from the front line in France and Belgium to the hospitals in Calais. By the end of 1918, the FANY was 400 women strong.

By the time WWII began, the FANY had expanded their operation considerably. One no longer had to be able to ride a horse but there was still a sense that the FANYs chose their recruits from a certain kind of family, under the old-fashioned notion that girls who had been sent away to boarding school would be of the "right stuff". Their unique constitution meant that unlike other service women, members of the FANY could be sent anywhere and do almost anything. That included packing explosives and working as spies.

Having learned all this and decided that it sounded suitably exciting, I wrote to the FANY at once, offering my services. Alas, the news came back that at 17, I was *still* too young even for this voluntary organisation. But on my 18th birthday – on the day itself – the FANY wrote back to me, asking if I was really interested. Was I ever! I was over the moon at the news. That letter from the FANY was better than any of the birthday cards I'd received that day. At last I was going to be able to do my bit.

CHAPTER THIRTEEN

Patricia

In the early autumn of 1942, after completing the interceptor training course in Southmead, I was sent to my first posting in Withernsea in the East Riding of Yorkshire. I'd never been to that part of the country before and I was very excited indeed to be heading for pastures new.

The original Y stations were established during the First World War. During the Second World War, most of those old stations were reopened and new ones were quickly set up along the East and South coasts. Some were temporary, with interceptors working out of large vans full of wireless equipment that could be moved from place to place as needed. Others were in plain old domestic houses that just happened to be in the right position. The Y station at Withernsea, just down the coast from Hull, had once been a boarding house called The St Leonard's Hotel. The Royal Navy had completely taken it over. We Wrens worked and lived in the house, which was right by the sea. A large bedroom on the first floor had been converted into a watch room, furnished with the all-important HRO radios, which were used to tune in to traffic in the Baltic and the North Sea. Other bedrooms had been made into dormitories (known as "cabins" of course) where we slept on the traditional bunks.

Withernsea was a relatively small Y station, which went by the naval name of *HMS Beaver* (though we never really called it that. We Y Service types were unorthodox for Wrens). The staff during my time there comprised 12 German-speaking Petty Officer Linguists and a couple of girls who didn't speak German but who were trained in Morse Code and wireless telegraphy. There was a Third Officer, who was in charge of the general running of the station. We were supported by one naval signal man who acted as our mechanic. His name was Mr Mason and he was also charged with teaching us Morse if we volunteered to study it, as most of us did, knowing that it would make us more useful. If we reached a certain standard, we would be sent back to Southmead to take an official course.

The Y station at Withernsea was a wonderful place to begin my career as an interceptor. It was a well-run station. I got on famously with my fellow petty officers and we all liked Third Officer Penelope Sparrow. I would make some good friends at Withernsea, though we came from a wide variety of backgrounds. Peggy Blakey grew up in Hungary, where her father had a business. Valerie Forsyth's family had a smart shop on Princes' Street in Edinburgh. We were all very envious of her beautiful shoes and handbags. We made a tight group though all we 12 young women really had in common was that for some reason or another we had all come to speak German fluently. As it happened, the kind of German I had learned – through informal conversation with Lilly and Edith – turned out to be more useful than classical school-taught German when it came to listening in on real live Kriegsmarine radio operators.

Naturally, the Y station had to be live 24 hours a day so we worked in four-hour shifts with a pattern of four hours on, followed by eight hours off, for four days in a row before we had a day's rest. Two or three of us worked each shift. I was surprised to discover that I didn't find it too difficult to concentrate no matter the hour, but the worst shift was definitely the one that began at four in the morning.

If you'd worked from eight to midday, the four in the morning shift came next. You would be woken at half past three and quickly dress in your jerseys and bell bottoms. We didn't have to wear full uniform at night and thankfully, because we lived as well as worked in the station, we didn't have a long commute. We just shuffled down the corridor from the bedrooms (cabins) to the watch room. The Wrens who had manned the previous shift would make us cocoa and fill us in on what they'd heard that night before handing over. A third or fourth Wren – there was always one on standby – would keep us supplied with the tea, coffee and cocoa we needed to keep going through the small hours.

When a shift began, we would sit down at a bench, stick on our headphones and begin to search the Kriegsmarine's known frequencies, just as we had been trained to by Freddie. It was simple yet laborious work. As Freddie himself said in a document which he sent to me in August 1990, while he was enjoying his retirement in Australia, "While it was known that the German vessels operated on certain frequencies, it was not known which frequency would be used on a particular occasion. To discover this it was necessary to search manually backwards and forwards across the dials. There was no easy way such as we have today of detecting activity and it was always a severe test of endurance and application to maintain a searching watch over a long period, especially during the hours of darkness when both mind and body are clamouring for relaxation." As one's mind and body definitely were at four a.m.!

At Withernsea, we were mostly listening for German motor torpedo boats (MTBs), which were known as E-boats, and destroyers, which were laying sea mines and attacking Allied convoys by night. We didn't pick up our own ships because they broadcast on different frequencies altogether, but quite often we would find Elbe-Weser Radio, a coastal radio station, or hear a German weather report being broadcast from a base on land. The German ships themselves stayed as quiet as they could for obvious reasons. They wished to remain hidden just as much as we wanted to find them. For a while, in fact, the Kriegsmarine had a policy of total wireless silence during operations but since that was just as inconvenient for them as it was for us, they soon began communicating with each other on VH/F channels again, working in the 30 – 50 m/c band.

Sometimes we would happen upon a "warming up" signal. Many of the German radio operators liked to switch their radios on long before they transmitted, which was helpful. If you heard that familiar rushing sound, you just had to stick on it until someone started talking as they inevitably would. When they did, you had to write down by hand exactly what they said. Exactly. If anything wasn't clear, you had to leave it out, rather than make a guess.

In Freddie Marshall's view, "In all forms of 'Y' or intercept work, experienced operators acquire something like a sixth sense concerning what is happening or about to happen. This is not or should not be imagination or speculation and it can be invaluable when added to the 'black and white' of the intercepted signals."

Many of the messages we intercepted were in plain German. When one of those came through, we'd keep noting what was said until the signing-off sign, which was QRUUD, came through. The Germans were very methodical and always gave signing on and off signs. At that point, we would hand the message over to our senior officer, who passed the text straight to our nearest naval base at Immingham, so that our own MTBs might be dispatched. The officer was on duty 24/7 and would have to be woken from sleep to make the necessary call if required. The phone was not in the watch room which, for obvious reasons, had to be as quiet as possible. We dare not miss a thing. Especially when the messages we received were in what we know now as Enigma code.

Enigma Code was one of the most effective encryption devices ever developed. It was generated using an Enigma machine, an early sort of computer, which housed an electromechanical rotor system that scrambled the letters of the alphabet according to settings that were changed on a daily basis. As the coder typed on the machine's keyboard, the rotors moved to transpose the original letters with that day's code. To decrypt a message in Enigma code, the receiving station had to use the same settings as the transmitting station, according to a prearranged schedule.

Enigma had been used prior to war by German banks and other commercial interests, who needed to keep customer information private. Now the German forces were using it extensively, convinced as they were that it was impossible to crack. Little did they know that Alan Turing and Gordon Welchman had been developing their own machine – the Bombe machine – which could decode Enigma as fast as the Germans could write it.

When an Enigma code message came over the airwaves, we had to write down the letters, then pass them to the officer who would have them typed up on a teleprinter and sent immediately to Bletchley Park. Of course, with the high levels of secrecy in operation at that time, we didn't actually know it was Bletchley Park or that what we were sending was Enigma code. We knew Bletchley only as Station X to our Station Y.

For the purposes of maintaining the utmost security, we were only ever given as much information as we needed to do our jobs and nothing more. There was little chance of us leaking any official secrets, because we really didn't know any!

The Enigma messages would however begin and end in plain language, with the operator asking their signal strength, for example. In general a strong signal meant that the transmitting vessel was close by, but signals could be reduced in strength by obstacles such as other ships or even by a heavy fog bank. Likewise, freak conditions might mean we heard messages from a very great distance indeed, such as happened when, thanks to weather conditions and the fact that ultra-high frequency signals were sent up into the ionosphere and dropped again at a distance, we picked up radio traffic from German tanks all the way over on the Russian front. There was also one particularly memorable time when another Y station nearby tuned in to a taxi control office in Budapest.

Thanks to such incidents, we had all come to know that the strength of a signal could be deceptive. As soon as we realised what we were listening to, we didn't follow it any longer but went back to looking for sea traffic. And from time to time, there were nights when we heard nothing of any interest at all.

We had the occasional visit from Freddie, who was keen to ensure that his "Fairies" were keeping up the good work, but there were sometimes visits by senior Wrens who didn't seem to properly understand what on earth we were doing, sitting in the watch room for hour after hour, slowly moving up and down the frequencies. We once had an inspection by a senior WRNS officer who asked, "If the reception's so bad, why don't you just ask them to send the signal through again?" Why indeed!

CHAPTER FOURTEEN

Patricia

My first few weeks at Withernsea were quite tiring as I got used to the serious business of being an interceptor, but it wasn't all work. In our spare time, Peggy Blakey and I helped Mr Mason to paint the station's greenhouse. We also got involved in the local community. We mucked in at harvest time and helped with the hay-making. Whenever there was an important local event, we were pressed into service as the village's only permanent uniformed residents. We often had to march through the town behind the enthusiastic boy scouts. Such marches usually descended into comedy, since none of us Wrens could ever seem to remember how to do a "wheel left" or an "eyes right" so long after our basic training.

One memorable day, one of the locals turned up at the station with a box full of tap-dancing shoes. It was an unexpected and unusual gift but we put it to good use. We quickly put the shoes on and set about choreographing a dance routine in the station's attic. A photograph taken at the time shows our impromptu chorus line outside the station itself. Silly things such as that kept our spirits high and contributed to the happy atmosphere.

On sunny days, we would bicycle to the lighthouse at Spurn Point. Commander Casson, the lighthouse keeper, would sometimes let us climb up to look at the view. I didn't much like walking around the very narrow walkway around the lamp − it never felt terribly safe to me − but the view was indeed spectacular.

Though there was a cinema nearby, there wasn't an awful lot else to do but walk and bike and practise our tap-dancing (though alas we never put on a show). On Sundays, the entire town was closed for the day, except for what I believe to have been one of Britain's first takeaway restaurants. There was a house with a hatch in the wall. Next to that hatch was a price list. You'd pass half a crown through the hatch to a hand belonging to an anonymous worker, who would in return pass a white plate full of food back out to you. You'd eat the food while standing outside, then pass the plate back. Though it was convenient, the food was usually pretty disgusting. There were lots of greasy chips.

Other adventures were to be had in nearby Hull. Hull was heavily bombed of course. We would hear the German bombers flying in over the Y station at night and pray for the people who lived and worked in the places they were heading for. But the city carried on regardless and throughout my time there the station hotel had quite a pleasant bar. I would go there to meet a friend of mine – a steady boyfriend, I suppose I'd call him now – a merchant navy radio officer, who was waiting to join a convoy. We had just about enough money between us to have a beer each as we talked.

My boyfriend and I didn't talk about work much. We each knew it was best not to ask rather than put the other in an awkward position. However one day he told me that every one of the men who had been on his training course had gone down with their ships. Every one. As he relayed their stories, I knew he was pretty sure he would suffer the same fate. When at last the time came for him to leave with his convoy, he promised me, "If I get to where I'm going and back, I'll send you a letter to say I made it." The letter never came.

Shortly after my merchant navy friend disappeared, I got another bout of bovine tuberculosis. This time, rather than being sent home to Newland Hall, I was sent to a hospital in nearby Beverly to recover. There I met another patient – a trainee RAF pilot. At that time, the life expectancy of pilots who went into battle was not very long at all, but this pilot could barely even get off the ground. His was an unusual predicament. Every time he flew his plane above a certain speed and then attempted a dive, he'd suffer a burst blood vessel.

While we were both convalescing in the same hospital, the pilot and I explored the nearby town together and became firm friends. He promised me that when he was discharged and back in the pilot's seat, he would fly over the hospital in my honour. He kept his word. One afternoon, I looked up to see him flying overhead in his training plane. He did a dive to impress me further. And before I knew it, he was back in the hospital again with yet another exploded vein!

Though I loved the romantic idea of having a boyfriend, the truth was that the war had its effect on the way we formed relationships then. Knowing that at any moment the person you'd fallen for could disappear forever meant that it was hard to get very deeply involved. There was a sense of *carpe diem* to everything, as is illustrated in this letter which I wrote to my mother shortly after I arrived in Withernsea. We were told we should not keep diaries lest details of what we were doing at the Y station fell into the wrong hands, but I wrote to my mother and to my sister Jean as often as I could. Poor Paddy Doumis…

St Leonard's
Friday

My own darling Mum,

Thank you so much for you long and funny letter…

…I heard from Paddy Doumis (an Irishman I met at Grosvenor House) this morning, he is in Kent, but determined to come up here when he gets a 48, and wants to fit it in with mine, when I get one. It's most annoying. I wish people didn't always think you mean more than you do. We did have rather a rapturous embrace in a secluded balcony at Grosvenor House, I must admit, but only in the way one does in a war, (all this, darling, as one girl to another over the hairbrushes), and goodness knows, if I'd thought he meant anything I certainly wouldn't have let him, not being the fast type. On the previous occasions (remarked Mme Dubarry, thoughtfully powdering her nose with the fuller's earth) it never has meant anything, so it's rather a shock to find Paddy continuing to yap on the trail.

Of course, in this arid waste, it would be more fun to have someone to take one out than not, and Paddy is very kind and quite congenial, but he just doesn't rouse any kind of a spark. And I'm afraid that if he spends his 48 and several months' pay travelling from Kent to Hull for the fun of entertaining yours truly, he'll begin to think he's raising not only a spark but a conflagration... I really don't want him to spend a lot of money coming up here, because I don't feel it's worth it. But I'm awfully bad at putting these things, and usually I'm so tactful that the more I try to discourage people the more encouraged they are. These impasses are, I am sure, all part of the misfortune of having been born with an absolute saccharinely kind heart or a soft head. Or something. Anyway, I must get down to the chilling-off process. By the way, the affaire Doumis is a revolution in so far as he's the first subaltern I've ever had to discourage!

The sea is so lovely. Every day it is different colours and all of them are completely satisfying. And the sunrises are glorious. It is full moon season at present, last night there was a huge gold moon making a great dazzle across the waves, and later all the foam was white in the moonlight. Today it is steel blue and there are heavy waves smashing in all along. Another girl and I are just going for a walk.

I've just been re-reading All Quiet On The Western Front. Gosh it is good. It's amazing that anyone who had read that could ever want another war. Of course it's probably over-vividly written but I don't know: probably the next generation will think the blitz-stories are over-vivid!

Bye bye for now, darling angel Mum.
Love from Pat

I wrote home often, though never about work. I knew I shouldn't be keeping a diary now that I was on active service but on 13 February 1943, I did make a few notes that characterised some of the frustrations of my time at Withernsea.

"It's certainly a beautiful day so far. The sun has just heaved itself out of a leaden sea, to the SE, and is pouring in my window (time 8.30). I've just come off second night watch and am just about to go to sleep till 1400 (unless the army start firing their bloody machine guns off into the sea bang under our windows, as they have a craze for doing: they've got a battle school on at the moment, and that's one of the toughening processes. (Much tougher, I may say, on us – who've been working for 5 hours or so while they were peacefully asleep – than on them)... I only got 2 hours' sleep before going on watch at 0330, and even when I have had enough sleep I feel sick throughout that watch. So I'm not going to stay up writing this long. I hate going to bed on such a divine day but if I don't it will mean only getting two hours sleep in 42 and if one does that one isn't much use by the end of the final 2330 – 0330 watch! So schluß for now!"

On one occasion, I was sent north from Withernsea to Scarborough for a few days with a colleague, where there was a large radio listening station. It was not one of our Y stations. It was staffed by men and women who searched exclusively for signals from U-boats, the German submarines, which broadcast on different frequencies to the traffic we followed. The powers that be were concerned that our Y Service might be missing some useful surface traffic within the range of Scarborough so we were to check those frequencies.

The Scarborough station was very different from Withernsea. It was no pleasant converted hotel. Instead, it was situated in a large hangar, camouflaged by turf, near the Scarborough Race Course. It was a very strange location. Inside the hangar, there were many listening positions. In the middle, the officer in charge had a desk on a platform. He had links to all the direction-finding stations on the coast. In the days before radar, direction-finding equipment, which relied on two separate stations being able to ascertain the position of the origin of a radio signal by triangulation, was the next best thing.

While my Withernsea colleague and I were there, we didn't hear any new German surface naval traffic, but the Scarborough interceptors did pick up a signal from a U-boat. Thereafter followed one of the most tension-filled experiences of my life.

You had to be fast to get a fix on a U-boat when it surfaced. As soon as this particular German submarine was picked up, the whole team sat in deathly silence, hardly even daring to breathe, while the officer on the platform gave the U-boat's frequency to direction-finding stations nearby. It was so important and very high stress. You could feel the tension in the air. In 1943, Allied convoys in the Atlantic were having a terrible time with the U-boats that prowled the sea like packs of wolves, picking off ships as they pleased. I knew how deadly the submarines could be and wanted to do whatever I could to help destroyers such as Uncle Tid's HMS Faulknor track them down. I don't know what happened to the U-boat we listened in to that day.

There was also talk of the possibility that some of us linguists would be sent to North Africa. A professor of Italian came several times a week from Hull University to teach us Italian in preparation. We never needed it. But having impressed Mr Mason with my Morse code skills, in the summer of '43, I was sent back to Southmead in Wimbledon for another course. When I graduated, I automatically became a chief petty officer, adding two more brass buttons and a couple of blue flashes to my uniform.

CHAPTER FIFTEEN

Patricia

As a newly minted Chief Petty Officer, I was sent to Lyme Regis. It was usual WRNS "Y" practice to keep people moving from place to place, presumably in order to prevent complacency and familiarity leading to a drop in standards. Thus every promotion meant a move.

I would be sad to leave my friends but all the same, I was pretty happy when I got my new orders. Withernsea had been a great introduction to my career in the Y Service but I was looking forward to learning and seeing more. I was also very much looking forward to being on the south coast, which I had hitherto known only as a holiday destination. Lyme Regis is the beautiful Dorset coastal town made famous by the John Fowles novel *The French Lieutenant's Woman*, which immortalised The Cobb – the town's harbour – with its old stone pier.

Many buildings had seen their purpose changed through the war. Before 1939, the Y station at Lyme Regis had been a golf club. You took the road up the hill out of town to the golf course which was set on a cliff. The extra height was useful as it meant we could hear messages from further away. It also meant that while it made for an easy bicycle ride into the town, it was a real slog to get back to the station afterwards.

The station itself was relatively small. There were just eight of us interceptors and a cook and a steward to look after us. There was no resident mechanic this time. We worked the same shift pattern as I'd worked before. Four hours on and eight hours off right around the clock.

At Withernsea, I'd listened to ships in the Baltic and the North Sea. From Lyme Regis, I could hear the naval traffic at the western end of the English Channel and up and down the Normandy coast. I could also hear the French lighthouses that had been taken over by the Germans, talking to each other and to the ships going in and out of Cherbourg. The lighthouses had call signs based on plants and trees, like Edelweiss and Violeta. They were not operating as normal, of course. They no longer shone their lights for the safety of all sea traffic at night and in bad weather. If we heard that the lighthouse was planning to put its beams on at a certain time, then we knew that more than likely a German convoy was coming through.

I heard much later that one of our West Country Y stations had a very disappointing experience having intercepted a message from one of those lighthouses. An interceptor in their watch-room heard a German lighthouse keeper talking to the keeper of a lighthouse further along the coast. He said that if the other lighthouse keeper looked out in an hour's time, he would see something interesting: those notorious German battle cruisers, The Scharnhorst and The Gneisenau, would be coming up the Channel.

Of course, the Royal Navy very much wanted to know where to find and intercept these Kriegsmarine monsters and the interceptor who caught the message and the officer in charge duly made sure that it was immediately passed to the relevant desk at Admiralty. If the information they'd picked up was correct, here was an incredibly important opportunity to put two of Germany's biggest naval assets out of action.

Alas, the message that Y station had intercepted and transferred with such diligence and alacrity went unnoticed. It was put into the in-tray of an officer who had already gone home for the weekend! By the time the message was read the following Monday morning, the Scharnhorst and Gneisenau had long since sailed up the Channel largely unmolested by the Allies.

I think this must have been the incident I had written about in my diary in 1942, while I was still at home in

Lancashire. The daring escape of those ships caused a great deal of upset at the time.

While I was at Lyme Regis, there was one incident, on an afternoon watch, when I thought I'd picked up a signal from a U-boat! I quickly realised this was highly unlikely – a U-boat in broad daylight, surfacing so close to shore in the middle of Lyme Bay – and decided it was a freak transmission. For a moment, though, I was very excited indeed.

Of course my work was still top secret. We Wrens were encouraged to wear our own clothes rather than our uniforms when we were out and about and if anyone asked what we were doing up there at the golf club, we simply had to say we "worked in radio". There was, after all, no hiding the radio masts and aerials, but we hoped the vague answer would put any nosey parkers off. If anyone guessed the truth, they never said so. Fortunately, most people understood by now that it simply wasn't done to ask someone what they were working at in wartime. As the posters reminded us, "careless talk costs lives". And, in terms that seem very old-fashioned today, "Be like Dad, keep Mum".

The station at Lyme Regis was run by Third Officer Chamberlain, who was half French. She was a very frugal officer who would insist that we girls use our spare time to pick blackberries when they were in season or try to cadge whatever food we could from our local friends to supplement our rations. The local people were very kind and generous towards us. They would have gladly given us their excess fruit and veg but it felt wrong to be asking for it so directly. Everyone was on rations, after all.

At least the lucky men in the Royal Navy had a weekly rum ration. We Wrens had no such privilege, but at Lyme Regis, one thing we were never short of was cider. A local farmer would deliver our order by tractor.

I made some good friends at the Lyme Regis Y station and we did have some fun. If we had the time and the weather was good, we'd visit our colleagues at Portland Bill for a picnic. When Italy capitulated and signed the Armistice of Cassibile on 3 September 1943, we dressed in heavy duffel coats and pretended to be wizened sea dogs for an impromptu fancy-dress party. The town of Lyme Regis itself had adopted a destroyer which was based in Portsmouth. When the crew came to visit, there was a whole week of great celebrations and dinners.

One of the girls had an admirer – a pilot – who would often fly over the station and dip his wings in tribute to his love. If the girl in question was working a shift in the watch room or asleep when her beau flew over, she had instructed those of us who were awake but not working to dash out and wave table-cloths to make sure the pilot knew she hadn't forgotten him. It was fun for the first couple of times but our friend's insistence on involving us all in her love life, and the fact that when she was awake and not working, she monopolised the telephone, eventually made her quite unpopular.

I spent three months at Lyme Regis over the summer of 1943. It was a beautiful place to be at that time of year. But soon I was sent off on another course. This time, I was going to learn direction finding, one of the most important skills an interceptor could learn.

CHAPTER SIXTEEN

Jean

Late 1942 and early 1943 saw a real shift in the direction of the war. In November, British troops overcame the Axis forces at El Alamein, putting some 50,000 German troops out of action. Since August 1942, the Germans had also been kept well occupied on the Eastern front, fighting the Russians for control of Stalingrad. The battle for Stalingrad was the largest in the history of conflict. It's estimated that as many as two million troops and civilians were killed or injured.

In February 1943, the Russians prevailed and took back their city for good. Stalingrad seemed a long way away from England but the German defeat there marked a turning point. It made us believe it might be possible to defeat Hitler at last.

I was still concentrating hard on the news from the Far East and the war with Japan. We still didn't know much of our father's fate. Our mother wrote to him all the time but rarely received a response. And when a response did come, it was only ever a Red Cross postcard printed with ready-printed lines of text that had to be crossed out to make a message. *I am well / not well.* Things like that. And it would be months out of date, which meant that all we could really deduce was that our father had been alive at the time the postcard was written. We knew how quickly the situation might change.

When my 18th birthday arrived, having received that letter from the FANYs, asking if I was still interested in joining up, I replied in the affirmative at once. First however, I had to undergo an interview at the FANY HQ, which was in the vicarage of St Paul's Church in Wilton Place, London, next door to what is now the Berkeley Hotel. I was advised by people who knew about these things that it was important to convey my seriousness and make it clear that I wasn't just looking for a good time. I duly made sure that I wore no lipstick or nail polish.

The interview seemed to go well but I was somewhat confused that one of the questions the interviewer asked me was, "Do you like crossword puzzles?"

I loved crossword puzzles. At the end of a day cataloguing Grandboffin's cows at Newland Hall, there wasn't much entertainment to be had. Reading, music and crossword puzzles were just about it. All the same, I was surprised, if not a little annoyed, to be asked whether I enjoyed puzzling at a military interview. I assumed the interviewer had just run out of things to say and was making polite conversation.

After I confirmed my interest in puzzles, the interview was quickly concluded. I then took a few tests which didn't seem to be testing any skills in particular. I suppose now that they were looking at my problem-solving ability. Shortly afterwards, I received a letter confirming that I had been accepted as a FANY recruit. Then, before I knew it, I was heading off on basic training.

The FANY's basic training course took place in a large house, called Overthorpe Hall, near Banbury. Arriving there by night, however, I wasn't sure where it was. For two weeks, we were drilled in marching, the illustrious history of the corps, first aid and Morse code. We also had to do a variety of menial tasks including cooking and cleaning. Each morning we had to sweep the grates and lay new fires in every fireplace in the house, of which there was quite a number. For many of the new recruits, who had come from a certain class of family and were used to having servants, such grubby household chores were not something to which they were accustomed. However, we all quickly learned that the ethos of being in the FANY was that we would do whatever we were asked to do cheerfully and without too many questions.

At the end of the basic training, we returned to London, where we slept in a dormitory at the converted rectory in Wilton Place. Thanks to boarding school, I was used to the dormitory life but there were some girls who weren't and they didn't seem happy with the arrangement at all. A couple of them left very quickly.

At this point we still didn't have uniforms since they were being made to measure. That didn't mean we didn't have to do daily drills. Each morning we marched in our civvies the short distance from Wilton Place to Hyde Park, where we were put through our paces. It felt a little silly to be marching about in civilian clothes, but we got on with it all the same.

When at last our uniforms arrived, we were all terribly proud of them. For me, one of the best things about having mine was that I could now attend for free the lunchtime concerts at the National Gallery. These concerts were organised by Myra Hess, a celebrated pianist, who believed in the uplifting power of music. People would queue right around Trafalgar Square to gain entry.

There was one particular disadvantage to being in uniform, however. Now we were properly attired, we had to salute officers whenever we encountered them outside. There were a great many officers in London at that time and it wasn't always easy to tell which were our seniors. It was much easier to dive behind a car and hide if you saw a likely looking military type coming. I became quite good at diving out of sight.

Now that I was in Wilton Place, the reason for the crossword question became clear. I was to be trained to be a code and cipher officer. When I wasn't marching around Hyde Park, I was to be taught how to use various coding methods.

The first was called "Playfair". It was invented by Charles Wheatstone in 1854 and was the first "digram" substitution cipher, meaning that rather than swapping one letter for another as in the most basic type of code, pairs of letters known as bigrams were encrypted together. This simple change made the resulting cipher altogether more difficult to crack, since by pairing letters there were 600 possible bigrams as opposed to 26 letters of the alphabet. Playfair used a 5 by 5 table into which was written a key word or phrase – this was known as the Playfair Square. All you had to do to decrypt the message was know that key word and follow some simple rules about the transposition of the letters.

It was relatively easy to get up to speed with Playfair and it required nothing more complicated in terms of equipment than a pencil and paper. It was used in the field to send messages during combat regarding imminent action. It was fast and just complex enough to give any enemy interceptor a headache. However it was not so complicated that it could be used to send critical information. The Germans also used Playfair, far more extensively than we did, during WWII. Though Playfair could be time-consuming when done by hand, Bletchley Park soon developed a method for quickly decrypting the messages.

Later, I learned how to use a more complicated, double transposition method, called the "One Time Pad". The One Time Pad cipher system was named after the pads of paper on which a random sequence of letters that formed the key to the code were printed. Each encoded message required two identical pads – one for the person or office sending the message and one for the receiver. Each message would be written using one new page from the pad – agreed in advance – which could be easily destroyed. Sometimes, a field agent's one-time-pad was printed on silk. In that case, instead of destroying a page, they had to cut away the relevant section. So long as the pads didn't fall into the wrong hands, it was an almost infallible encryption technique.

With these skills under my belt, I was sent on my first posting. I was to be working at the SOE – the Special Operations Executive.

CHAPTER SEVENTEEN

Jean

The Special Operations Executive was formed in 1940, through the bringing together of three secret organisations, upon the orders of Churchill himself. The purpose of the SOE was to coordinate espionage and reconnaissance work in occupied Europe and South-east Asia. It also provided support for local resistance fighters. Upon its inauguration, Churchill is reputed to have ordered his new team to "set Europe ablaze".

The SOE was controversial. It was colloquially known as Churchill's Secret Army or, by those who were suspicious of its work, the Ministry of Ungentlemanly Warfare. And I was going to be working there! It was all very exciting.

Before I could start work, I had to sign the Official Secrets Act. Like Pat, I was a little taken aback by the penalties the Act laid down for those who dared to breach it, but, unlike Pat, I was not afraid of being asked to parachute into enemy territory. I think I would have relished it. That was not on the cards but I was at least glad that now I knew for sure I would not spend the war working in a kitchen. You didn't need to sign the Official Secrets Act to do the washing up, surely? I felt more important than I had ever felt before as I proudly signed my name.

In November 1943, I moved into another London house which had been taken over by the FANYs and started my new job. Each morning I took a bus to Baker Street, which was where SOE headquarters was based in an anonymous-looking office building with no plate on the door, though as a cover it was called the ISRB, the Inter Service Research Bureau. Another nickname for the SOE was "the Baker Street Irregulars".

To help preserve the anonymity of the SOE's offices, my fellow FANYs and I had been told that when travelling to work, we should always jump off the bus a stop earlier or a stop later than we needed to and complete the journey on foot. It was a ruse that didn't work especially well, as I discovered when one waggish conductor shouted, "Any more spies?" as our bus reached the closest stop.

But while SOE's location wasn't as secret as it might have been, what went on inside the building definitely was. I was given a cover story to tell anyone who asked me what my war work involved. I was to say that I worked in "personnel relations and training". I'd received an early lesson in the importance of being able to keep a secret when I was ticked off by an officer for talking indiscreetly while travelling in the back of a lorry with my fellow FANYs. "You never know who's listening."

The office where I worked was large but bare. It had once been a sitting room and still retained a grand fireplace but other than that, there was nothing but a few tables and chairs inside it. No machinery. All the equipment I had was a pad and pencil. It was all I needed. Messages came in via teleprinter and were handed out to us coders randomly. Everyone mucked in. There was no hierarchy. You simply took the next message off the top of the pile and got to work on it.

I was especially good at unravelling messages when, as sometimes happened, the agent in the field had deliberately corrupted a message because there was a particularly high risk of their pad falling into the wrong hands. Such messages were known as "indecipherables". It gave me an enormous amount of satisfaction to see the incomprehensible screeds of letters begin to make sense as words. It was far more exciting that doing a crossword.

At this time, London was still suffering bombing raids. One morning, while I was taking the bus to work, the air-raid sirens sounded just as we reached Marble Arch. The driver stopped the bus at once and we passengers all piled off to head for the nearest air-raid shelter, which happened to be in the Marble Arch tube station. In the confusion on the street, I ran down the wrong entrance and found myself face-to-face with a very dishevelled old man wearing a long dirty mac. He made a grab for me. I shrieked and ran straight back up to the surface and headed into Hyde Park. The prospect of bombs was far less frightening.

I hid in the park until the all-clear sounded, then got back onto the bus.

Soon it was December. Though there was still much to be worried about, the girls in the office were looking forward to Christmas, when several of us would be going home on leave. We were all homesick and very keen to see our families again. I had never been away from Newland Hall for so long.

I remember one particular evening, a couple of days before Christmas Eve. We were all in high spirits as we tidied our desks at the end of the day. As we larked about and discussed our Christmas plans, Leo Marks walked into the room.

I didn't work with Leo Marks but I certainly knew of him. Marks headed up the codes office that supported resistance agents in Northern France. The son of an antiquarian bookseller, Marks had been passionate about coding since childhood so as soon as he was called up, it was obvious that he would make a particularly useful cryptanalyst.

At the beginning of the war, famous poems and Bible passages were often used as encryption keys for agents in the field. It was Marks who pointed out that using well-known passages made the coded messages vulnerable, since the enemy was likely to recognise the passages and therefore have a better chance of guessing the key. The solution was to use new poems that were written in house. Marks soon came to head up a staff of 400 coder poets.

That December afternoon, Marks had been up on the roof and he brought with him the whiff of cold air as he stepped inside our office. We wished him a Merry Christmas.

"It's not a merry Christmas," he said. "Europe is burning. People are dying out there." And he launched into a passionate speech.

By the time Marks had finished, the happy mood had disappeared altogether and several of us were actually in tears. We later learned that Marks had heard that day that his girlfriend, Ruth Hambro, had been killed in a plane crash. Deranged with grief, he'd gone up to the roof with a view to throwing himself off and joining her in the afterlife.

On Christmas Eve 1943, Marks wrote a poem in Ruth Hambro's memory. It was called "The Life That I Have". It's a melancholy poem that speaks of undying love. Despite the poem's very personal origins, Marks allowed it to be used by the SOE. It was given to Violette Szabo, a beautiful French / British field agent who also happened to be a member of the FANY. Of the 50 female agents who were sent into France during WWII, 39 were FANYs. 13 of that number were killed.

On her second mission, Szabo, who was renowned as one of the best shots in the FANY corps, found herself in a fierce gun battle to provide cover for another agent. She was captured only when she ran out of ammunition. Her colleague escaped. Szabo was subsequently tortured by the Gestapo and eventually taken to the notorious concentration camp at Ravensbruck, where she was executed as the Allies closed in on the Germans in 1945. Years later, a film was written about Szabo's life – *Carve Her Name With Pride* – and the poem Marks had written in the aftermath of that miserable December night became famous all over the world.

I returned to Lancashire for Christmas in sombre mood, but there was some good news. In the few weeks I'd been at the SOE, I had already seen much more of life than I ever would have been able to had I stayed at Newland Hall, but I wanted to go even further afield. Having seen a notice asking for volunteers to go overseas, I'd jumped at the opportunity.

At Christmas, I learned that my application to be transferred overseas had been accepted. I was on the list. I told Mama and Grandboffin while I was home on leave. I don't think I expected Mama to be especially pleased, but I had not expected her to be so firmly opposed to my going overseas as she was. Since I was still only 18 and the age of majority was 21, I had to have her permission to go and she was determined not to give it. Not while Pat was at the other end of the country and our father was still goodness only knew where. She didn't think that she could stand to have me so far from home as well.

Fortunately for me, Grandboffin, to whom I had always been so close, understood how important it was for me to spread my wings. Taking my side, he somehow managed to talk my mother round and by the time I went back to London, I had, if not Mama's blessing exactly, then at least her agreement that I could take up an overseas posting if I really wanted to. When I asked her why she had changed her mind, she told me, "Because you were such a nuisance." Her one stipulation was that I should pack one good formal dress so that I would be ready for any parties. Even in wartime, standards must be kept high.

CHAPTER EIGHTEEN

Jean

In the New Year, I returned to the SOE and continued with my cipher work while I awaited further instructions. Now that I was on the list, I knew that I could be going overseas at any moment but had no idea where to. Even when the call came to say I should be ready to leave in a couple of days, I still didn't know my destination. I might be going to one of the most dangerous places on earth. I was sent to get a vaccination against yellow fever, which seemed ominous.

There were people from all sorts of different backgrounds working at the SOE – both servicemen and women and civilians. Leo Marks later referred to Baker Street as being "pitted and pockmarked with improbable people doing implausible things for imponderable purposes and succeeding by coincidence." But I enjoyed my time there among the boffins. I felt as though I had been doing something important to bring the war to a swift conclusion.

On the day of my departure, with my heart in my mouth, I joined a group of soldiers at a train station in West London that was reserved for troop trains. I did my best to stay jolly as I took in the enormity of my decision. I was about to leave the United Kingdom for the first time in my life. As the train headed north, I guessed that we must be on our way to Liverpool, the port from which our father had left for Singapore.

I guessed correctly. We arrived in Liverpool – where I drank the worst cup of tea of my life. It had been stewing all night – and we boarded a ship. I still had no clue where that ship was headed but having received a lightweight summer uniform, I was confident that it was at least going to be somewhere warm.

The ship was a former cruise liner – the MV Stirling Castle of the Union Castle Line – which had been requisitioned and repurposed as a troop transport. I was thrilled to discover that as an officer I would be travelling in first class (albeit in a cabin shared with five others). After a couple of uneasy early voyages, since September 1943 it was decreed that all FANYs being sent overseas should be ranked as cadet ensigns and given officer status.

We ensigns had one shoulder pip and a maroon cloth bar on our uniforms. I don't think the bona fide senior officers who travelled with us were all that pleased to see us. Especially since there was no alcohol to be had on the ship to make it less onerous to be sharing their space with a bunch of excitable young women on their first big adventure!

I'd received a letter from my commander on 12 January telling me about the promotion, "I am appointing you to the rank of Ensign temporary war rank w.e.f. 3.1.44." I sent that letter straight on to Newland Hall, asking my mother to keep it safe for any future great-grandchildren. In the same envelope I sent my little brother my remaining sweet coupons, since I would not have use for them now that I was going overseas. I wrote to him too. He'd recently acquired some new pets which I hoped would make up for the absence of both his big sisters and the fact that he was about to go off to a new boarding school.

STS. HQ
Room 98
The Horseguards
SW1
13.1.44

My Darling Old Bob,

This is, I'm afraid, good-bye for now, but not, I expect, for so very long. I hate leaving you, darling, but it does seem rather a pity to miss seeing all the things I shall see, and doing all the things

I shall do, and we'll have so long to be together when I get back.

I do so hope your Common Entrance goes off OK – I'm sure, actually, that it will. HAVE YOU LOST THAT RABBIT YET? If you have, may you fail! So what!

Pat says the canaries are lovely. I do hope they throw a rainbow-coloured egg and not just a fit when they realise who their owner is. I've been going to all the most expensive hotels in London – lovely! I don't know how much I've spent, but it's pounds. (Is Grandboffin listening? Shush!) I'm an officer now with a pip (red) on each shoulder. I'm an ENSIGN (= 2nd Lieut). Coo!

Well, honey, so long. I do hope you love Shrewsbury and do write if you have time. God bless you, my own darling brother,

Your loving Jinks.

The very next day the Stirling Castle set sail. With a destroyer escort, we headed first in the direction of the Irish coast, where we picked up a convoy of smaller vessels. From there we headed into the middle of the Atlantic.

Life on board took a little getting used to. The beginning of the voyage was rough and it was very cold in the Atlantic. There were frequent lifeboat drills to prepare us for the possibility of an emergency and we were quite restricted with regard to our movements about the ship. We had to stay below deck during the hours of darkness both for our safety and for the sake of our reputations. Neither were we allowed to exercise or do PT on the open decks during daylight hours in case we distracted the gunners. The only women who were allowed to do PT were members of the ENSA, the Entertainment National Service Association, who could often be seen doing ballet exercises around the ship.

The ENSA were very important. The association was formed in 1939 by theatre producers Basil Dean and Leslie Henson to provide entertainment for Allied troops wherever it was needed. Dean and Henson were able to rope in some very famous faces, including Vera Lynn, Tommy Cooper and Sir Laurence Olivier, to join ENSA at various times during the war.

The ENSA team on the Stirling Castle put on nightly entertainments to keep us all from getting too bored. There were also recitals of "light" and "heavy" music. "Heavy" referred to the classical music which was my personal prefer- ence. It didn't sound heavy to me! Though some people joked that ENSA stood for "Every Night Something Awful", I very much enjoyed their performances. There were also film shows and dances. Since the ship was "dry" we all used to queue for our sweet rations, even the colonels. We couldn't have wine but we could have a Mars Bar.

From the middle of the Atlantic, we turned south. I thought of Daddy and wondered if I would be following his journey to South Africa and thence to the Far East. That wasn't the case. As we reached the bottom of Portugal, the ship suddenly turned left, tacked along the south-western coast of Spain, and, shedding most of the vessels in our convoy, slipped through the Strait of Gibraltar into the Mediterranean.

It was an eerie experience. I knew that U-boats still prowled the Mediterranean on the hunt for allied ships, so I felt a rising sense of excitement but also of danger. For this momentous occasion, we were allowed up onto the deck with the men. To the north, Europe was entirely dark except for a single light shining from the rock of Gibraltar. To the south of us, however, the North African coast glittered. There was no blackout there. It was beautiful to see Tangier in Morocco all lit up like a Christmas tree. As I watched the Atlas Mountains passing by, I marvelled at how life there carried on, regardless of the War which had engulfed the whole of Europe.

That night the sea was calm but our voyage through the Mediterranean was not entirely without event. As we sailed close to Malta, a U-boat was spotted nearby and the alarm went up. Though we had left behind our convoy, we were still being accompanied by two destroyers. They went straight into action. They circled the Stirling Castle like a pair of sheepdogs and let off depth charges. When a torpedo was set off, we all raced to the rail at the edge of the deck to watch it go. We had to be told to get back as we were unbalancing the ship. When the excitement was over, I turned to see members of the ENSA calmly practising their ballet exercises as though nothing momentous had happened.

All was quiet again, but our destroyer escorts continued their sheepdog act until we made it safely to port.

Approximately two weeks after leaving Liverpool, the Stirling Castle docked in Alexandria, where we FANYs disembarked. I had never imagined as I turned 18 that less than three months later I would be in Egypt! I was overwhelmed by the sights and sounds and smells that greeted us in the busy, bustling port. I took in the palm trees, the men in their long white robes, the women dressed head to toe in black. There were goats, donkeys and mules. There were even camels.

From Alexandria, we went by train to Cairo, which offered us the perfect opportunity to see more of the country. The train carriages were small, so we left our cases in the corridor to give ourselves extra space. That was a big mistake. While my friends and I were busy looking out of the carriage window as while we waited at a tiny local station, someone slipped onto the train and stole my bag. So much for my mother's insistence that I pack a party dress! The thief left me with nothing but the clothes I stood up in.

We were to be billeted on a base in Heliopolis – the ancient "city of the sun" – seven miles to the east of the capital city.

These days, Heliopolis is full of skyscrapers, but in the 1940s, it was just a village on the edge of the desert. There was still sand between the houses. As we got closer, I wondered what the base would be like. In London, I'd lived in a house that had been converted into FANY dorms. A base sounded very different.

The base at Heliopolis was quite formal. We were always in uniform. The accommodation was very good. At the centre was the mess in a big villa. We were put up in smaller houses nearby. The nearby garrison church gave services in English. The clergyman in charge there was from Lancaster so we soon became friends and I was often invited to tea. It felt safe enough but we were reminded daily that we were not on holiday. For the short walk from the mess to our living quarters, we were always accompanied by a local guard for our protection. We had transport to take us to and from Cairo itself, which was half an hour away. If we missed the official transport, which was a rather unglamorous three-ton truck with wooden benches nailed down in the back, we had to take a tram. Always the white tram and not the brown, we were instructed. Only the white one was safe. If you missed the tram, the next choice was to hire a carriage, inevitably pulled by an elderly horse that looked like a bag of bones. I felt very sorry for those horses.

Our office was on the banks of the Nile in central Cairo. Like Pat's Y station, it was manned 24 hours a day in shifts. A shift was 6 to 8 hours long, depending on the time of day and the volume of work. There were days when we were so busy we would have to go straight from one shift into another without a break. In Cairo, we FANY coders were working principally with the underground resistance in mainland Greece, in the Baltic States and in Crete. We also relayed mainline traffic regarding Egypt to London and to other offices in North Africa. We did a certain amount of work with boats, getting agents in and out of occupied areas of Southern Europe. We received their messages via a signal office which took them down as Morse code.

In Cairo, I came to recognise certain codenames and had a real sense of the agents in the field as individuals that I perhaps hadn't had when I was in Baker Street. I became increasingly aware of the importance of deciphering messages that had "gone wrong" and were corrupted, since they meant that the agent was likely to be in danger and needed backup.

Unfortunately, the Cairo office was situated right next to a hospital incinerator which smelled very nasty in the heat, though I was warned that the January temperatures were not excessively high and it would only get worse as the year wore on. Some of the girls hung flowers at the windows in an attempt to sweeten the air. Night duties were rather horrid because of the smell.

But when I wasn't near the hospital with its stink, I found I loved the heat, which was unlike anything I had

ever experienced before. Everything in Egypt was so new
and different to me. After three years of rationing, it was
heaven to be somewhere where there were no restrictions
whatsoever on what we could buy with our wages. There
were sweets everywhere, in huge colourful piles on market
stalls. I thought of poor Bobby back in England and wished I
could send him a bucketful. And of course I was able to buy
some clothes to replace those I lost on the train.

When I wasn't working, I made the most of my free
time, approaching Egypt rather like a pre-war tourist. I had
a four-day break upon arrival, during which I joined a group
of American servicemen for a tour. They took me to see the
pyramids.

Closer to the base, we spent relaxing days at the Gezira
Sporting Club, which was situated on an island in the
middle of the Nile. It was a true oasis, kept watered and
green in contrast to the surrounding countryside. One could
play golf, tennis or squash there, or just take a swim in
the pool. Naturally, one would never risk swimming in the
crocodile-infested river. We also got a little taste of Europe
at Café Groppi, which had a well-kept tea-garden. Café
Groppi was founded by a Swiss pastry chef and had a reputation for excellent cakes. In fact, they were so good that our
commanding officer had to set a rule that we FANYs were to
be allowed no more than one visit to Groppi per week – at

which we were to eat only one cake – to prevent us getting upset stomachs. Hygiene was an important discipline. There were some interesting-looking places where we were simply not permitted to eat.

There were fortnightly parties in the FANY mess, where we were allowed to discard our uniforms and dress up. Those parties were very popular with the servicemen stationed nearby. Other nights off were often spent going to Cairo's luxurious hotels and nightclubs. That was not without its danger, however. Egypt's King Farouk I, who was notorious for his lavish lifestyle, had a terrible eye for the ladies and we'd been warned that if he made up his mind to get to know a particular woman, nobody could stop him. We heard tales of ATS girls who had found themselves in terrible trouble with Farouk and learned that the best way to avoid any unpleasantness was to avoid catching his eye in the first place. So, we set up a system, whereby if Farouk was spotted entering a club, we FANYs would immediately leave via the backdoor, even running through the kitchen if we had to. The club and restaurant owners were only too happy to assist our escape plans. Once we were safely out of Farouk's range, we'd go on to the next club. Poor Farouk must have wondered why every club he entered was empty of pretty young women. Life in Egypt was not a bit like being at a sheltered girls' boarding school! Not that I wanted to alarm my mother when I wrote home…

Ensign J Owtram FANY
ME95
MEF

12th Feb. 44

My Own Darling Mummy,

I wonder if you have got my last letter yet. I believe they take ages to get through. Yours haven't come yet, but I've had one from Pat. I'm having a marvellous time still, and have met lots of awfully nice people. It's such a change from knowing no one really. Today is Sunday (13th) and 3 of us went to early service at the Garrison church down the road. It was a lovely light church in the camp and we had breakfast in the recreation room above afterwards. Everyone was so nice and friendly and it was all quite informal – the Padre, a major, a 2nd Lt, several privates and a sergeant all getting us tea and sandwiches!

Now I'm sitting on the verandah in the sun. We go on again at 1.30 today as we came off at 12 last night. This system of shifts is rather exhausting but gives us quite a lot of time off. I saw the pyramids (by moonlight!) the night before last. They were very impressive tho' useless. It's really amazing how big the stones are, great chunks of rock piled up symmetrically away up in the air and all in perfect proportion and the shape's marvellous. It really is a triangle and looked as if it was cut out of cardboard from a little distance. There's one big one and lots of little ones round. I'm going again in daylight, preferably on a camel, to see inside.

It was Farouk's birthday on Friday and all the streets were decorated with their green and white flags. Even the trams had flags on their bars! We hoped Farouk would be at the Auberge de Pyramides where we went on, but he wasn't. We went to Mena House for dinner, which is where Churchill stayed when he was here. It's a lovely place. The conferences with Stalin and Chiang Kai Shek were held there too. Yesterday we had lunch at Gezira Club, which most of us belong to, with our 2 airmen on leave who are very sweet and rather fun. My friend, Bill, is Scotch and a pet. All my friends off the boat seem to have moved on now which is sad. Give my love to everyone won't you, we only get one air letter a week to send so I can't write to them all. Could you explain this please? All my love to you darling, and Pat, and Bobs, and God bless.

Ever your loving Jean xxxxx

In another later letter, to Pat and Bobby, I described the weather in Heliopolis. "*It rains about once in two years for a whole day and about three times a winter for 20 minutes. When it does, if it isn't much, the locals put white hankies over their fezzes, as umbrellas. When it's a lot they get ready for the end of the world. We had a hamseen which is a hot dry wind off the desert, all last week, it brought a solid curtain of fine sand with it and everything's still covered. You could draw pictures on all your books and tables and shoes and even on your pillow each morning, with the shutters shut all night. And if you went out your eyes and hair and mouth got full of it and you had to do some dredging, almost, before you could eat! It's horrible, and goes on for at least three or four days every so often. At night it turned cold, just like an English wind..."*

In the end, I spent just a couple of months in Egypt. It was a wonderful experience. I loved my work there and I loved getting to know something of a truly different culture to my own. I was a very long way from Lancashire in all respects. But after a while I began to tire of the bumpy open lorry journey to the office by the far-from-fragrant hospital. I disliked the cockroaches and the ever-present risk of dysentery and the desert wind that covered everything with red dust. That wind – the khamsin – had come as rather a nasty surprise to me. I also wanted to see more of the world. My desire to travel had been awakened, so when I was asked if I would like to go to Italy, I said "yes" at once.

CHAPTER NINETEEN

Patricia

Training in direction-finding took my career to a higher level again. In the days before radar, direction-finding using specially calibrated aerials was the best way of working out the position of an enemy vessel. We Y interceptors would work out which direction a signal was coming from by following it until it faded. If another station picked up the same ship, we could triangulate its position using both our readings.

Like Withernsea, the Y station in Lyme Regis did not have direction finding equipment so once I'd qualified, and become a Chief Petty Officer in the process, I was sent to Abbot's Cliff at Capel Le Ferne in Kent.

The large white house at Abbot's Cliff, which went by the naval name HMS Lynx, had been a private home before the war. It was set on the edge of a cliff midway between Dover and Folkestone that looked directly over the Channel to Cap

Gris-Nez, which was just 23 miles away as the crow flies. The coast was often foggy – Capel Le Ferne's nickname is Capel Le Fog – but on a bright day, you could sometimes see flashes of sunlight reflected off the windscreens of cars over in France.

HMS Lynx was the furthest south-east of the Y stations and the closest to Europe, and as such it was by far the busiest. It was the biggest station I'd worked in, and its importance was underlined by the fact that here a First Officer rather than a Third Officer was in charge. Not all the Wrens spoke German. Those that didn't could still take down Morse Code, which was the same in any language. And the station had direction-finding equipment, of course.

Because the direction-finding aerials were different from those we used to listen in on naval traffic, they were set on a different building, which had to be at some distance from the watch room so that the two types of radio reception would not interfere with one another. At Abbot's Cliff, the direction-finding kit was kept in "The Tower", which sounds far grander than it was. The Tower was in fact a simple round wooden hut, shaped like a windmill with no sails. It had no windows and was rather cold and lonely.

Only one person at a time was on watch in the Tower. At least for a Tower night shift, one didn't have to wear full uniform – bellbottoms and a warm jersey were the norm. When one was on the night shift, one could even sleep until a phone call from the watch room alerted one to the presence of a ship that needed immediate tracking. Then it would be a fast scramble out of bed to the equipment.

The aerials outside the hut had feeders that connected to a direction-finding goniometer – which was a circular bar – and wireless receiver inside. You had to swing the goniometer around until the signal faded and note where it happened. It was always easier to judge the fade of a signal rather than an increase in strength. Down the coast, another direction-finder would hopefully be doing the same thing to give the triangulation point. You had to be quick since, cognisant that they might be tracked, the German ships were under strict instructions to transmit for no longer than 30 seconds at a time.

In November, I wrote to my mother, letting her know how I was getting on and including details of my rather inauspicious arrival at my new posting. Never let it be said that I didn't how to make a striking first impression!

Folkestone 2075

Abbot's Cliff House,
Capel,
Nr Dover,
Kent

Chapter Nineteen

2/11/43

My own darling Mum,

Thank you so much for your letter…

    Abbot's Cliff is a great success so far – it is the place to be, and I think I shall love it. I had a nice weekend at Chatham, which included a Hallowe'en Party which was rather fun, and got here on Monday morning. Well, then, of all the unfortunate things to do, I must have been attacked by a gastric flu germ because while I was being shown around I suddenly went completely faint – which I never do – and collapsed, and then was awfully sick. However, everyone was perfectly sweet, I was never more fussed in my life, and they all thought it must be the sight of A., because the last person did the same thing. So I spent the afternoon asleep on someone's bed, and then got up full of joie de vivre and was at once sick again, however, it seems to be passing off though I don't quite feel settled yet, though nothing – touch wood! – has happened so far today. But isn't it maddening? I always was unfortunate!

    I will tell you all that has happened so far. I arrived at Dover and was met by a transport, and we went up to the castle and down to the Dockyard on errands, which was fun. Apparently the gun-duels go on fairly regularly – it's really absolutely babyish, whenever one side starts the other has to retaliate to maintain its prestige, but apart from hurrying through Dover market-place (and, I suppose, Calais market-place!) one needn't take much notice. Dover has a very front-line atmosphere but isn't really as mouse-eaten as everyone expects.

It rained all this morning, and the Channel was all clouds, and then about teatime it suddenly cleared, and there was all the coastline of France – you can imagine the thrill! On clear days one can see houses, and the clock-tower at Calais – oh boy!

Yes, I shall be a CPO, but it hasn't come through yet. I'm so glad you're pleased about it darling – so am I, and people don't always realise! I did wish you'd been here when I was feeling sick, however sweet other people are it is never the same. But this really is a nice station, and masses of dances and awfully nice people, and being sick on arrival is such a success I think I shall repeat it at arrival on every subsequent station!

The house is pretty ghastly, everything rattles unceasingly in the gale and I'm in a large untidy room on the ground-floor with six other people, but as they're all very nice the doss-house atmosphere doesn't matter! Anyway, what does anything matter when one can see France from the window?!

Tons of love darling – Pat

I made good friends at Abbot's Cliff, though once again we were all from very different backgrounds and might never have had the chance to meet in peacetime. When I first arrived at the station, we often travelled up to London in our time off, but as D-Day drew closer, we were set a strict 20-mile limit for our wanderings and had to content ourselves with Dover, Folkestone and Canterbury. As usual, we had to keep our work a secret from the locals. Some of my colleagues were told that if they were asked what they were doing, they were to say they were factory girls from Kent enjoying a holiday!

When things were quiet, some of us Wrens learned unofficially with the Military Police to use Sten guns. We were shown how to take the guns apart and reassemble them before taking target practice. I think Abbot's Cliff was the only Y station with such a guard. The military police had been posted there to defend us from any commando-style raids. The British were undertaking such raids on the French coast and so it was assumed the Germans must be planning the same for our south coast. In such an event, we thought it might be useful to know how to use a gun. We also had regular evacuation drills and received instruction on how to disable our radios rather than have them fall into enemy hands. One such practice, at another station, nearly ended in disaster when the commanding officer forgot to declare the exercise a drill. Luckily, the Wrens were interrupted just before they set fire to their equipment!

Sometimes we went to Cerne, about a quarter of a mile away, where the interceptors of the WAAF listened in to a different kind of enemy traffic. The Luftwaffe bombers overhead had no time to code their messages, which we passed straight to an RAF intelligence centre. We often heard things like, "Achtung Indianer links!", which meant "Look out. Indian to the left!" In what they thought of as a sky-borne game of Cowboys and Indians, the Luftwaffe had cast the RAF as the Indians.

We were also occasionally sent to help out the Wrens who were in the Dover casemates, a series of offices and rooms that were dug into the white cliffs. The casemates were built in the 18th century, to repel an invasion by Napoleon, but they were significantly extended during WWII and a great many people were working there. The Wrens here were different from the ones I'd met before. They were career Wrens and, if I'm being candid, they had the intimidating demeanour of prison officers.

There was a church on top of the cliffs near the casemates. I remember going to a service there at Christmas. Down below, Dover was completely dark in the blackout. It was at such melancholy moments that I missed home and, in particular, my father, very much indeed.

Dover was very heavily shelled by the Germans and as D-Day approached that shelling only became more intense. If we had time off and were in Dover when we heard the shelling warning – a double air-raid alarm – we had to get straight back to the base. Unless, that is, we were in one particular restaurant, called the Crypt, which was safely underground. If we were there, we could stay and finish having dinner.

Folkestone was shelled less often, so when we weren't working, we tended to go there. Sometimes we'd be offered a ride down the long hill into the town on the back of a despatch rider's bike. It was no mean feat to ride pillion in a tight skirt while juggling tricorn hat, shoulder bag, library books and the tin hat you were required to have with you always.

One treat that some of us Wrens very much enjoyed was finding a riding school in Hythe where the regular clients had gone off to join the forces and the horses needed exercising. We could ride them for free if we would take them up on the Downs for a canter. After a night watch in the stuffy watch room it was such a joy to canter along on a well-trained horse in the clean fresh sea air. We also found a local café in Hythe which could provide rolls and honey for after our ride before we returned for a well-earned sleep.

There were lots of troops stationed in Kent in the run-up to D-Day. Occasionally we would join the Free French at their club in Folkestone to listen to music and watch French films. It made a nice change from listening to German. The Free French seemed very homesick and were keen to get the operation to retake northern France underway.

Meanwhile, pilots from the nearby RAF stations would sometimes fly to Dublin and bring back supplies to help our parties go with a swing. While I was at Abbot's Cliff, I took my first ever flight with a friend from the Fleet Air Arm's search and rescue team. He took me up in the observer's seat of a plane called a Walrus. Though I was frozen stiff, I was thrilled to see the towns on the coast laid out like model villages as we flew up and down the Channel. I'm pretty sure that my friend wasn't meant to be taking Wrens on joyrides. The Wren in charge of my Y station certainly didn't know.

I had another friend, a Canadian army officer nicknamed "Black" who had access to a staff car. When neither of us was working we'd explore the coast and occasionally Black would let me take the wheel.

I'd learned to drive while I was in London, taking lessons from a British School of Motoring instructor based in Battersea. As we drove around the streets of south London, he would inevitably direct me towards Lavender Hill near Clapham Junction and to one shop in particular where, he cheekily assured me, "Most of my students like to buy me a packet of cigarettes".

Still, he got me up to speed with my driving and it certainly came in handy at Abbots Cliff, where I became the designated driver on the Wrens' nights out. Needless to say, I wasn't very popular when, at the end of the evening, I went around the parties extracting my friends so that we could get back to the base before the deadline. It wasn't much fun to have to break up the revelry. Neither was it much fun to have to drive a truck along the country lanes during the blackout, with only a small space in the windscreen to look through. But I always managed to get everyone home safely.

From Abbot's Cliff, which I believe is the nearest house to France, we had a front-row view of the Channel. As I've said, on a clear day, we could see all the way to Cap Gris Nez and the French coast, even to the clock tower in Calais. It was very strange to think that Europe was completely cut off from us when in reality we were so very close.

We saw lots of the preparations for D-Day. We watched convoys of empty landing craft being moved into position. We also saw a section of one of the Mulberry Harbour – temporary floating harbours, which would service our supply ships – being hauled towards Portsmouth. We had no idea at the time what they were. They looked like upside-down tables with long spindly legs.

Listening in to the Germans from Abbot's Cliff was sometimes much harder than it had been at Withernsea or Lyme Regis. Though the German warships warming up their radios in Boulogne and Calais harbour could be very loud and clear, occasionally our Y station had so much ambient noise that it was difficult to hear the signals we picked up. Not for nothing was our section of the Channel known as

Hellfire Corner. German bombers often flew right overhead. Nearby was an American anti-aircraft unit. Once, a naïve young Wren came strolling into the watch room with an unexploded shell, saying "look what I've found!" It was from the American anti-aircraft unit. Shouting "Take it away!", we dived under our desks and remained there until the shell was removed and made safe.

One sad day, we watched as a German gun hit a merchant ship, which was part of an Allied convoy, right beneath our cliff. The ship exploded and burst into flames. We saw no-one escape. The convoy had to keep moving westward with a gap in it, leaving the ship drifting alone. It was a moment none of us would ever forget.

CHAPTER TWENTY

Jean

At the end of March 1944, I left Egypt for Italy. I had arrived in Egypt by sea. I would be leaving by air. It was to be my first time in an aeroplane and I was very excited indeed, particularly as, by happy coincidence, the pilot was someone whom I had met on the long voyage from Liverpool to Alexandria.

The plane was a big heavy thing, an army transport. We left Heliopolis Airport in the early hours of the morning in total darkness. I gripped the edges of my seat in fear as the plane gathered speed and lifted into the air but as soon as we reached cruising height, I forgot all my reservations. By the time we arrived in Benghazi for breakfast, I felt like an old hand at this flying business. I saw the sun rise twice on that short hop. Once over the desert as we took off from Egypt and again as we landed on the coast of Libya.

Thanks to my pilot friend, I was invited into the cockpit as we flew on towards Malta, our next stop, in the glow of dawn. It was thrilling enough to be invited to see the cockpit at all. I had not expected to be asked if I would like to take a turn at the controls.

Of course, my friend wasn't going to let me take over the plane entirely, but I was allowed to sit in his seat alongside the co-pilot – who retained overall control – and hold the yoke. The men gave me some rudimentary instruction – along the lines of "Don't press that button" – and showed me how to waggle the wings up and down. I had a wonderful time, doing my best to keep the plane on an even keel, as it were. I began to think that perhaps I should have joined the WAAF.

I thought I did rather well for a first-timer but, as I went to retake my seat in the main cabin for landing, I couldn't help noticing that several of my fellow passengers looked a little green. As I sat down, the man in the seat next to mine asked, "Did you notice how bumpy it was back there? Terrible turbulence." I shook my head, though of course I knew that it wasn't turbulence he'd felt at all! I thought it best not to explain.

With the professional pilots back in charge, we landed safely and smoothly in Malta to refuel and to give everyone a chance to settle their stomachs before we flew on again to Brindisi in Southern Italy.

I will never forget what it was like to fly towards Brindisi that beautiful spring morning. The landscape was spectacular. As we flew low over the Apennines, all the almond trees were in full blossom. The white flowers looked like confetti on the branches. After the arid Egyptian desert, it was a very welcome sight and I think I already knew that I would fall in love with La Bella Italia.

Landing in Brindisi was altogether less hectic than the arrival in Alexandria and I was glad to hear that our base – the HQ SO (M) Admin Echelon, Military Establishment 57 – was only another half an hour away by road towards Bari. I was to be stationed in Torre a Mare, a small fishing village, where a number of houses had been taken over by the Royal Corps of Signals. I would be joining several other FANY coders and wireless operators in a new, purpose-built signal building. Torre a Mare was also home to a supply base and a parachute packing station.

Of course, Italy had been on the same side of the war as Germany until its capitulation in September 1943. Benito Mussolini, the Fascist dictator the Italians called Il Duce, had formed an alliance with the Nazis back in 1936. Hitler and Mussolini had very similar ambitions. In 1938, Mussolini supported Hitler's annexation of Austria and introduced anti-Jewish laws of his own on Italian soil. In June 1940, he entered the war on the German side, with the intention of taking advantage of the situation to expand the Italian empire in North Africa and the Middle East. Unfortunately for Mussolini, the Allies prevailed in North Africa and in January 1943 the Allied leaders met in Casablanca, where they formed a plan to strike back at the Axis powers by invading Italy, which Churchill called "the soft underbelly of Europe".

The invasion, code-named Operation Husky, began in Sicily on 9 July 1943. By 8 September the Italians had surrendered and Mussolini was in prison. But while the Allies were preparing to storm the Italian mainland, the Germans moved to occupy Italy themselves. There was another month of fierce fighting before the Allies reached Naples and liberated southern Italy, which promptly declared war on Germany.

When I arrived in Italy, the Germans were still in Rome and Mussolini had been reinstated as puppet leader of the Italian Social Republic, the German-occupied north.

Despite this recent history, the locals in Puglia were immediately warm and friendly towards us newcomers. They were always happy to stop and chat and help me to improve my Italian. It was only ever small talk, of course. I knew better than to talk to anyone about my work – we weren't actually supposed to fraternise with the locals at all – but there was genuine warmth in the way they treated us. After all, they hadn't had such a great time under the Fascists or the Germans, who ruled through violence, taking young Italian men into forced labour and meting out terrible and sometimes deadly punishment to anyone who demurred. In March 1944, Italian partisans planted a bomb in Rome which killed 33 Germans. 335 civilians were shot in retaliation.

My first billet, the Villa Anna I, on the road out of Torre to Noicàttaro, was pretty but very basic. I soon learned that there was no hot water on tap. I'd have to boil a kettle. To get enough for a bath involved gathering fuel by picking up driftwood from along the coast until you had enough to light a fire under the very temperamental boiler. Then you'd have to pray that the water supply wouldn't get cut off in the middle of the process, leaving the boiler empty but dangerously overheated. The whole rigmarole wasn't something anyone had the time or the inclination to do more than once a week. It was far easier to take a quick trip to Bari for a bath at the officers' hotel, the Imperiale, where we FANYs sometimes clubbed together to take a room for a night or two.

But apart from the water issues, which were par for the course in war time, there were a great many reasons to enjoy being in Torre a Mare as the spring bloomed all around. Getting back to base from the Cairo office had always been something of a slog and could feel quite dangerous at times. In Italy, I could walk back to our little house along the beach late at night or early in the morning, feeling wonderfully free as I marvelled at the beauty of the ever-changing colours of the Adriatic sea. On hot days, I might even jump in that sea to cool off. The Villa Anna had a flat roof which was perfect for sunbathing.

In the house next door to our digs lived a little boy, aged between two and three, who liked to look out for us FANYs as we came home at the end of a shift. When we were able to get sweets, we always saved some for him. We occasionally shared food with the adults too. Nobody had much but everyone was glad to share what they had, including hot water. I remember coming home dusty from a walk along the dried-out riverbed, where I'd been looking for wild flowers. One of our Italian neighbours insisted on preparing a bowl of warm water so I could wash off my feet.

In the evenings, we would sometimes join the locals to attend a concert or see an amateur opera performance. We always knew when it was going to be Puccini's *Madame Butterfly* because the little boy next door would be washed and dressed up for his walk-on role as Butterfly's son in act three. Gino, the cook at the FANY mess, was a big fan of Puccini and would sing extracts from *Tosca*, *La Bohème* and *Madame Butterfly* at the slightest provocation. As a music lover, it was wonderful to find myself in a place where everyone seemed to appreciate good music, though I was shocked the first time I heard heckling from the gallery when the musicians on stage played badly!

I enjoyed not only classical music but popular music too. I soon learned to sing *Lili Marlene* in Italian. The very German love song, popularised by Marlene Dietrich, was a big hit all over Europe.

Puglia itself was very lovely and I enjoyed exploring the local towns and villages. I especially loved the charming cone-shaped Trulli houses. The little white homes, built for the local shepherds, seemed to me as though they wouldn't be out of place in the pages of a book of fairy tales. The Puglian countryside was stunning and seemed to be always full of flowers, as I wrote in a letter to Pat as my first spring there became summer. *"The flowers up in the valley now are just Paradise. I spend my leisure hours up there, in an atmosphere of honey and buttercups and sun. The 'valley' is a sort of dry gully with a stony floor and steep sides covered with luxuriant foliage and multiferous flowers. Mainly a sort of tiny cyclamen, very transparent mauve with red tips to the petals and grows on the ground (not in a flowerpot, as you might expect) on short stems… I counted 14 different kinds of flowers up there yesterday. Cyclamens, crocii (yellow and mauve and tiny little ones), dog daisies, real daisies, buttercups, baby narcissae with a heavenly smell, dandelion-things and various little ones I don't know. And all very hot and sleepy and blue sky and quite hot again, sort of St Luke, or Mark or somebody's summer."*

CHAPTER TWENTY-ONE

Jean

But Italy was not all playtime.

Though the Allies were still fighting their way up the country, the role of the office to which I'd been posted was to support resistance fighters directly across the Adriatic in the Balkans. Previously, the Balkan resistance had been under the auspices of Cairo, but now that southern Italy was in Allied hands, it made much more sense to move our operation closer so that messages could be sent and received more quickly and more reliably. Likewise, it was much easier to move supplies to the Balkans from Italy rather than via Greece.

There were many complications with the resistance movement in the Balkan region, where occupation by Axis Forces had effectively sparked civil war. Yugoslavia had tried to remain neutral when war first broke out, but eventually signed the Tripartite Pact with the Axis powers in March

1941. It was a move that outraged several Yugoslav air force officers, who quickly seized power in a *coup d'état*. In response, the Axis forces invaded Yugoslavia in April 1941, after which it was swiftly broken up and shared between the Germans, Italians, Hungarians and Bulgarians.

The two main resistance groups in Yugoslavia – the Communist Partisans and the Chetniks – had fought side by side in the Uprising in Serbia in 1941, through which they created the largest liberated territory in occupied Europe, but since then despite their joint cause they had been riven by infighting.

The Chetniks, led by General Draza Mihailovic, were loyal to the King of Yugoslavia, Peter II, who was exiled and living in London. The Communist Partisans were led by the charismatic WW1 hero Josip Broz, known to all as Tito due to his habit of delegating duties by saying in his local dialect, "Ti to, ti to", which meant "You do this, you do that".

In 1941, when the two resistance groups had worked as one, the Chetniks were more numerous but the Partisans were more disciplined. They also had very different philosophies which meant they could not agree on a unified command or strategy. The Partisans believed in nothing short of all-out war against the occupying forces and thought that the destruction of property and civilian deaths were a price worth paying for freedom. The Chetniks were more pragmatic. They wished to avoid civilian casualties at all costs, and were prepared to come to an accommodation with the enemy to achieve their aims.

Unsurprisingly, the Partisans began to suspect that the Chetniks were betraying them to the Axis occupiers. Indeed, the Chetniks had collaborated with Italian forces until the Italian capitulation. The Partisans were also unimpressed by the Chetniks' loyalty to their exiled king, whom the Partisans considered to be dodging his duty by going into hiding in London, though he had been just 17 years old when the Germans marched in (Poor King Peter had further alienated his subjects by marrying Princess Alexandra of Greece and Denmark. It was considered unduly frivolous for him to be celebrating a wedding while Yugoslavia was at war). It wasn't long before the rift had gone too far and any further collaboration between Partisans and Chetniks was impossible.

In the summer of 1943, Churchill had sent Fitzroy Maclean into Yugoslavia to report on the situation. Maclean was a former diplomat, who resigned his position in order to be able to serve in the army during the war. Freed from his diplomatic duties, he enlisted as a private in the Queen's Own Cameron Highlanders and quickly rose to Brigadier before becoming a member of the fledgling SAS. A good friend of Ian Fleming, Maclean is said to have been the model for James Bond. He also happened to be the Conservative MP for Lancaster, my home constituency. Though our Uncle Bill

ABOVE LEFT Major Owtram before going to the Far East, 1941. **ABOVE RIGHT** Dorothy Owtram, née Daniel, served in the Women's Land Army in WW1. **BELOW** Newland Hall, our family home.

TOP Patricia and Jean as children, 1920s.
LEFT Nanny rowing us on the lake.

ABOVE Patricia Jean & Robert ('Bob'), 1930s. **ABOVE RIGHT** Amelie Getzl – known to all as Amy. **RIGHT** We loved dressing up in costumes from the dressing-up box, 1930s.

ABOVE Fishing on a Scottish loch on our last holiday, 1939. **BELOW LEFT** Patricia wth her father, 1941. **BELOW RIGHT** Jean, Dorothy, Patricia and Bob around Cary's embarkation, 1941. **BOTTOM RIGHT** Our caravan.

ABOVE LEFT With our father away, Grandboffin teaches Bob to shoot. **ABOVE RIGHT** Jean and Dorothy, 1943. **BELOW** Jean, Bob and Patricia at Newland Hall, January 1944.

ABOVE Patricia, Chief Petty Officer Wren, 1944. BELOW LEFT Jean, S.O.E., Italy 1944. BELOW RIGHT Patricia wearing her own devised Battledress, a dyed greatcoat with badges – 'no one objected!'

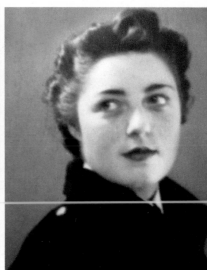

OVE The family reunited and photographed by Patricia the day after Colonel Owtram's return home. L to R: Col. C.J. Daniel, Bob, rothy, Cary, Jean and Co. H.H. Owtram, October 1945. BELOW LEFT Patricia at the BBC, 1960s. BELOW RIGHT Patricia with her parents Newland Hall, 1980s.

ABOVE Patricia is awarded Legion d'Honneur Medal in 2019 by the French Ambassador, Jean-Pierre Jouyet.
LEFT Patricia and Jean look over their photos.
BELOW Patricia and Jean in Patricia's Garden, 2020.

had had Maclean, whom he referred to as "Fitz", with his campaign, I knew the man only by reputation at the time I came to be working with the Yugoslav resistance from Italy. It was as a result of his mission to Yugoslavia that Maclean had advised Churchill the Allies should concentrate on helping Tito's partisans.

Thus the traffic my Italian office received was largely to do with keeping Tito's people supplied with everything they needed: machine guns and ammunition, medical supplies and sometimes food, which was dropped in by parachute. Those parachute drops were a dangerous business, since the Germans soon cottoned on to what was happening and often lit decoy fires to fool our agents into dropping supplies and themselves in exactly the wrong spot.

Meanwhile, there continued to be in-fighting within the resistance and there were frequent situations where our embedded agents had to be withdrawn, lest we armed the groups with whom they were liaising to fight against each other and thus inadvertently ended up killing our own people! There were casualties and they had to be brought out in a hurry. It was often very tense. One dreaded hearing the worst, so we did our very best to get the messages we decoded and encoded absolutely right.

My work in Italy felt more personal than it had done in Egypt. We were sending and receiving messages from individuals and sometimes those messages bordered on flirtatious. I remember the first line of a poem which one agent used to identify himself was, "I wish I were a woolly worm with furs upon my…". You can imagine the sort of correspondence that ensued. It was also sometimes possible to get to know agents in person when they had shore leave. It made the work we coders did both more interesting and more difficult, adding as it did a layer of tension. It was always difficult to hear that an agent had been killed or captured. Even harder when you could put a name to a face. You might have danced with them at a party. You might, as some of my colleagues did, have fallen in love.

In September 1944, I wrote to Pat, telling her, *"…here in Southern Italy you see quite a lot of Jugo Slav Partisans, with just the red star to distinguish them. They're on the whole just as you expect them. Very strong jaws and tragic eyes and dark and quiet. The girls all have straight hair on their shoulders. A partisan officer saluted me once and as it's what I always want to do to them it was a little overwhelming. I do think all these underground people are the most terrific thing ever."*

From time to time, we even got a visit a from Tito himself. Though none of us were supposed to know when the Partisan leader was in Italy, he was given away by his dog. Tito always insisted that his dog travelled with him and we all came to recognise the huge German Shepherd, who was called Tigger, when we saw him being walked around the town. We pretended not to know who the famous dog's owner was, of course.

We were kept abreast of the situation all over the rest of the world through *The Union Jack*, a forces newspaper, and through a daily bulletin which was delivered by an officer each morning at a sort of assembly. These "morning prayers" as they were called weren't compulsory, but if you weren't on a watch, you would try to attend. There was also the "war room". The Army had taken over a whole building in Bari and for a while the signals office was moved there. The "war room" was an almost empty room dominated by a large table with a huge map spread out upon it. Every day, a piece of string representing the front in Italy was moved to represent the progress being made. There were strict rules about who could move that piece of string, as I said in a letter to Pat:

"Did I ever tell you about our office map and the little notice attached? It says, 'Please do not touch the battle line. It will be pushed forward every morning by Lt Wright', who is a quiet little two pipper and a base wallah. Humorous, I think. It is now ornamented by our slogan, "Good show", which is cribbed from a WAAF we once had who greeted every fresh catastrophe with 'Good show, Sergeant'."

There were plenty of small and large catastrophes in Italy in 1944 but I quickly learned the importance of retaining a sense of humour and being able to say "Good show".

CHAPTER TWENTY-TWO

Patricia

In the late spring of 1944, while Jean was settling in to her Italian posting, I had a very interesting encounter. I'd just finished a night watch in the direction-finding tower. After so many hours in that room, I was glad to get some fresh air as I opened the door. As was usual for a night shift, I was dressed in my bellbottoms and a jersey. Thus I was not wearing my proper uniform when, to my surprise, I saw a small group of army staff officers, or so I thought, walking towards me.

As the men drew closer, I did a double take. The man in the middle looked extremely familiar. I'd just come off a very intensive shift. It was still only eight o'clock in the morning. Perhaps I was just dreaming or perhaps... Perhaps the man in the centre of the group really was Winston Churchill!

As he drew nearer, our prime minister was unmistake-able. He wasn't smoking a cigar but in all other respects he was exactly as he appeared in the news reels. Winston Churchill, our prime minister. And he was flanked by Field Marshal Bernard Montgomery, Monty, commander of all Allied ground forces, in his distinctive black beret.

As soon as I realised I wasn't dreaming, I was faced with a dilemma. The rule was that you saluted senior officers but only when wearing a hat. Because I'd been on a night-shift in the direction-finding tower, I was not wearing my hat. So I did the best I could. I gave them a wave and said "Good morning!" They replied "Good morning!" and walked on. I couldn't wait to tell my colleagues who I'd just seen.

Much later I heard that Churchill was seen in the Dover area at least five times in the run-up to D-Day. His visits were part of Operation Fortitude, a complicated plan to mislead the Germans with regard to the Allies' intention to invade Northern France. Churchill and Monty were meant to be seen and their presence near Dover reported back to Berlin via German spies as proof that the Allies had their sights set on Calais. Radio transmissions containing fake information leading to the same conclusion were broadcast for the same purpose. The Allies even created a "phantom army", a modern variation on the old Trojan Horse, to wrong-foot the German generals. The "First US Army Group" was an entirely fictitious platoon, overseen by American General George Patten. The platoon's tanks were in fact inflatable decoys but once covered with camouflage nets they looked real enough to the German spy planes that overflew them where they had been carefully positioned to be noticed.

The German spies were very efficient. They reported all the misinformation the Allies fed them back to their commanders and Operation Fortitude was a success. The Germans did divert some of their troops away from Normandy.

D-Day – the first day of Operation Overlord – was a long time in the planning. Northern France was very heavily defended by a series of fortifications that the Germans called the Atlantic Wall. Some 2,400 miles of bunkers, pill-box towers and landing obstacles edged the German-occupied Atlantic coast all the way from south-western France to Scandinavia. The Germans had also planted more than 500,000 landmines on the beaches and armed Calais itself with three huge gun batteries. And of course the Channel was still patrolled by the Kriegsmarine. All these things had to be taken into consideration. A practice D-Day drill called Operation Tiger, wherein US troops rehearsed a beach landing on Slapton Sands in Devon, not far from my previous posting, ended in disaster when the Allies' rehearsal convoy came under real torpedo fire from German E-boats in Lyme Bay.

However, there were weaknesses in the German ranks that could be exploited. The great German general Rommel understood the importance of extra defences in Normandy and wished to keep a Panzer tank division on permanent patrol near the coast there. He was overruled by Hitler, who demanded that the tanks be stationed near Paris instead. Hitler's refusal to listen to his military experts would greatly contribute to his downfall.

We knew D-Day was imminent when, on 4 June, First Officer Anne Walker went in to Dover Castle to collect sealed orders. D-Day was originally planned for 5 June but had to be postponed due to weather conditions in the Channel making it too difficult for the landing craft to put to sea. On 5 June, First Officer Walker returned to Dover Castle for fresh orders.

As we now know, that bad weather turned out to be a blessing. The Germans assumed that they could rest easy for another day, but the Allies took advantage of a weather forecast that showed a brief lull in the stormy conditions overnight. The German bombers were grounded, and presumably assumed the same of the RAF, but some British planes were able to take off in the early hours of 6 June. They dropped dummy paratroopers rigged with explosives behind enemy lines. Others dropped record players that broadcast the sound of a large invasion. They were followed by a pre-dawn bombing raid by 1,000 RAF bombers. And after them came the largest amphibious invasion in history, as nearly 7,000 Allied ships and landing vessels carried 156,000 Allied infantry to the Normandy beaches.

I was asleep when Operation Overlord swung into action and the D-Day landings finally began. It was four o'clock in the morning when one of my colleagues raced round the cabins and woke those of us who were in our bunks by shouting, "It's started!" The watch room was full of senior naval officers. If we needed any clue of the importance of that day, this was it.

Some of the Wrens at Abbot's Cliff had husbands or fiancés who were involved in Operation Overlord. One of my friends, Pam Mackan from Bristol, was especially relieved to hear that the Normandy landings had started. Her fiancé Geoff was a prisoner of war in Germany and she was thrilled to know the Allies were on their way at last.

It was a misty sort of day, grey and chilly in the early morning. I remember we watched a convoy of empty landing craft going down towards Portsmouth to join the second wave. After that, there was no news for hours on end. Just like everybody else up and down the country, we had to tune in to the BBC to hear what was happening. It was all tremendously tense as we thought of the young servicemen, whom we'd met and laughed with at dances and parties over the past few months, parachuting or sailing into unimaginable danger. For quite some time we didn't know whether the landings were a success or a disaster.

We know now that the Allied infantry landed on five separate beaches, codenamed Utah, Omaha, Gold, Juno and Sword. The Americans, landing on Utah beach and Omaha, suffered high casualties as they sailed straight into German sniper fire. The British and the Canadians had better luck and were able to quickly take a couple of bridges. The Germans were caught sleeping, quite literally. They had just 50,000 infantrymen in Normandy at the time and though it was clear that they needed reinforcements, no-one dared wake Hitler to ask for them! Hitler's insistence on ultimate control tied his generals' hands. While the Führer slept on until midday, as was his habit, the Allies took maximum advantage.

By 11 June, all five beaches were under Allied control, allowing the deployment of another 2.5 million servicemen via the Mulberry harbours we'd seen being moved into position. The Mulberry harbours also enabled the landing of 500,000 tanks and other military vehicles and millions of tonnes of supplies. With this back-up in place, the Allies were able to liberate all of Northern France by the end of August, opening up the long-awaited Second Front and striking a killer blow to German dominance in Northern Europe. Without a doubt, the Battle of Normandy was a turning point, though it cost 225,000 lives.

I turned 21 two weeks after D-Day. By then, we knew for sure that the Second Front had been opened and the Allies were making headway, so it felt as though we could afford to celebrate. I joined forces with a couple of friends who had birthdays around the same time to have a small party to mark my coming of age. But the war was far from over and it wasn't long before the Germans had unleashed a new weapon upon us. The V1s.

When I first saw a V1, I had no idea what it was. It looked like a very noisy comet with a fiery tail, straight out of a medieval painting. We soon came to realise that the V1s became a real danger when that fiery tail went out and they stopped making the whining noise that had quickly earned them the nick-name of "Doodlebugs" or "Buzz bombs" (their German name was "Vergeltungswaffe", which means "Vengeance Weapon"). This sudden silence meant that the rockets had run out of fuel, at which point they would drop like stones from the sky and detonate, causing much destruction.

The V1s were relatively short-range missiles, fired from the Normandy Coast, often right over our roof. They were mostly aimed at London, but Dover was a target too. To combat the new menace, the Allies launched Operation Crossbow, defending Britain's cities from the V1s with a mixture of anti-aircraft guns and fighter planes. When a V1 bombardment began, RAF fighter planes – Spitfires and Hurricanes – would fly out to intercept them, gently nudging the V1s with the tips of their wings so that they were sent off their planned trajectory and fell harmlessly into the sea or onto empty ground. Between the guns and the fighter planes, around 80% of the V1s were disabled before they found their targets.

Ironically, the only near miss we experienced at Abbot's Cliff came not from a V1 but from friendly fire. Right next to our Y station at this time was a battery of American anti-aircraft guns. While they tackled the V1s, an American shell fell outside our watch room. Thankfully, no-one was hurt, but our commanding officer quickly had the guns moved further off. Quite apart from the danger of shells gone astray, there was little point having a Y listening station rendered deaf by the racket of Allied artillery.

It was a very noisy and nerve-wracking summer. It was never easy to sleep after a night watch.

CHAPTER TWENTY-THREE

Jean

Of course, my colleagues in Italy and I were delighted to hear the news of the D-Day landings but in June 1944, we had good news even closer to base. The Eighth Army, the field army made up of infantry divisions from all over the British Empire − from Australia, New Zealand, South Africa and India in particular − finally entered Rome on 5 June. Two months later, on 4 August, they were in Florence.

August 1944 was a very busy month at the station in Torre a Mare. There had been rumours that the Germans were preparing to pull out of the Balkans to divert their resources to holding northern Italy. During one of the Partisan leader's visits to Italy, Fitzroy Maclean and Tito had cooked up a plan to ensure that if the Germans did decide to implement such a withdrawal, very few German soldiers would make it out in one piece.

The plan, which was called "Operation Ratweek", was for seven days of coordinated attacks by the Partisans, with Allied air and sea back-up, on the German lines of communication in Yugoslavia. Enemy-held bridges and viaducts would be blown up. The railways, which the Germans would likely use to move their troops north en masse, were the most important targets.

In the run-up to Ratweek, my office was kept busy round the clock coding and decoding instructions regarding special drops of extra explosives and ammunition for the Partisan teams on the ground and plans for air support from the Balkan Air Force, based in Bari, which would be needed as soon as the Germans realised what was going on. As the excitement began to build, people who were due to be on leave requested a change of date so that they could be there as Ratweek happened. At the end of August, Fitzroy Maclean flew to Bojnik in Serbia in preparation.

Ratweek began on 1 September. The Partisans' efforts, combined with fighter attacks by the BAF and bomber raids by the 15th USAAF, who made more than 1300 sorties in their Flying Fortresses, destroyed much German military hardware and caused a significant amount of damage to the road and rail infrastructure in Yugoslavia. At the same time the Royal Navy launched missions on the Dalmatian coast. By the end of the week, the Partisans had taken control of eight communication centres and 49 railway stations. They had destroyed 97 bridges and almost 50 miles of railway tracks. They'd cut another 50 miles' worth of telephone and telegraph lines. In addition, more than 4,000 Axis soldiers had been killed, 2,000 injured and over 5,000 captured. The German withdrawal had been comprehensively hampered, just as planned.

Ratweek was deemed a success but in the months that followed, the Allied relationship with the Partisans began to sour, as Tito saw his chance to consolidate his power. As Tito flew to Moscow to negotiate with Stalin, it was becoming clear that the Allies and Tito had very different visions for a post-war Yugoslavia. Tito's vision included taking back Trieste, the hotly contested city on the Italian-Yugoslavian border. He'd told Fitzroy Maclean of his intention.

CHAPTER TWENTY-FOUR

Jean

When I wasn't on duty, I made the most of my time in Italy. Now that the Germans were in retreat, the country was opening up.

I often went to Naples and Sorrento with my fellow FANYs. We would either hitch a lift on an army lorry – British soldiers were always happy to offer us girls a seat since there were so few of us around – or go to the nearest RAF station and see if we couldn't pick up a ride in a small plane from there. On a number of occasions I hitched a huge distance just to see an opera as I described in this letter to Pat in the spring.

"Yesterday Jean Heller and I got a lift on Arthur's truck going north as far as Foggia. There we hopped a jeep and full colonel and driver to where the road divides, ½ going to Benevento and ½ to Avellino and Napoli. We got another jump with a sweet Suid Afrikan to N and were deposited on the YWCA doorstep. We then shot round Naples getting opera tickets and trying to contact Arthur who hadn't arrived and to fix up transport back

for the morrow. Finally we went to the opera solo and it was quite heaven. The Masked Ball *by Verdi, and the most lovely music and costumes and scenery and everything. The San Carlo is of course reasonably far famed. Gigli is singing there tonight! Which naturally we have missed.*

We sat in the gods, it cost 30 lire which is 1/6. Then we met Arthur at the Patria Transit Hotel and all went back to the YW and Arthur played the piano till we were thrown out. So Jean and I, having missed dinner, ate hard-boiled eggs and chocolate in our bedroom. This morning we met A. at 9 at the Patria to see him off (he's going North alas. He is, by the way, our ex-CSO and a honey). I'd bought 2 fluffy dogs, patented Neapolitan too, so we had one each and Jean got one too and we had coffee and waited for lifts. Arthur's truck broke down so he finally saw us off.

We had 2 jeeps to Foggia, the second with a charming Jewish captain called Denis Jacobson who gave me a driving lesson, and whisky and coffee in Foggia. We hitched him in Avelline and all went to a café there and sat round a table on the pavement in blazing sun and drank vermouth and coffee and ate sandwiches and cream cakes for lunch. Lovely! We finished the 70-odd miles home on the back of an open lorry and as I am now on night duty I've about had enough.

The mountains looked like those Alpine Xmas cards, jagged snow covered above new green valleys and sheets of flowers and blossom. It was so lovely it made me want to howl. Oh darling you must come here in the Spring, there's nowhere like the Apennines now. It's very hot and smells of honey in the country. But imagine going almost 200 miles at home (and back) to see an opera! And not even having fixed transport. But was it worth it."

If we could hitch a lift to a station, travelling by train was inexpensive and easy. I wrote to Pat about the Italian railways, which still had their German Reichsbahn livery: "*It always gives me a bit of a thrill to see Köln and München and Ludwigshafen and Königsberg on them*".

At this time, my letters home were generally about the landscape and the weather and Pat responded in kind. We also wrote about the books we were reading and the music to which we listened. I was trying to learn Italian by reading books I already knew, such as Daphne Du Maurier's *Rebecca*, in the language. There was an army library in Bari, from which I was able to borrow English language books, but I was always grateful when Pat was able to send me books from home. We all enjoyed *The Life and Times of Archy and Mehitabel* by Don Marquis, which followed the comic adventures of Archy the cockroach, who had been a poet in a previous life, and Mehitabel, an alley cat. Pat and I both loved the books of Margaret Kennedy, author of *The Constant Nymph*, which had been made into a film in 1943.

Occasionally, our letters mentioned romance. Many of the FANYs in Puglia were embroiled in exciting romances. With so few Allied servicewomen in Italy at that time, we were in high demand and there were always lots of dances where one could meet romantic prospects. Several of my friends became engaged as a result.

I didn't have a steady boyfriend but I did become good friends in a platonic way with an older man, Eric, who had access to a car. Like me, he was keen to see as much of Italy as he could, so we made several day trips together. I found it much easier to be friends with more mature men who didn't have any expectations of our friendship. The younger ones were always trying to seduce us FANYs and get us behind a hedge!

Being overseas and access to copious alcohol led many to leave the usual high standard of behaviour behind, as I complained in a letter to my sister after one hair-raising encounter, *"Last night I went out with a naval type to the club in Brindisi and we had a very good dinner and danced and then he started getting gooey and I had the hell of a time on the way home, and as I was sleepy. Anyway I got very browned off and altogether it was a bit much of a bad thing. I do wish that men didn't always assume that if they take you out they can then kiss you whenever they choose. I don't know if they're the same at home, it may just be the demoralising atmosphere of anywhere overseas. Everyone's morals just go by the board here if they're not careful. There's too much chance to do as you choose. Public opinion and convention aren't such a bad idea really!"*

I think perhaps I had deeper reasons for not wishing to have a boyfriend than wanting to preserve my reputation. Though at times in Italy we felt almost as though we were on holiday, the fact was, we were at war. It was hard to take the risk of giving one's heart to someone who might go off on a sortie and not come back. For some people, that risk intensified their need for romance and they threw themselves into short-lived relationships. Me, I felt the opposite. I wanted to protect my heart.

Of course, I still didn't know what had become of my father. As a family we knew that the only way to cope with the uncertainty was to try to carry on as normal, but there were moments when I felt great sadness as I wondered if I would ever see my father again. It must have been terrible for our mother but she didn't believe in self-pity. While I was in Italy, back at Newland Hall our mother took in several evacuees from Manchester and Liverpool. It didn't last long, as the poor children were so horribly homesick that their parents decided it would be less traumatic to have them back in the city.

Stark reminders of the reality of war were always with us even on those sunny days in Italy. I remember hitching a lift on a troop transport. We stopped to help a local driver whose lorry had broken down. As an engineer got his vehicle going again, I used my best Italian to ask him what he was transporting.

"Corpses," he told me. "Dead bodies."

It was in Italy that I learned to drive. I had driven some of the farm vehicles back at Newland Hall but the jeeps used by my colleagues were very different from tractors. I didn't have any formal lessons, however. The first time I got behind the wheel of a jeep was when I was crossing the Apennines with a friend. He was very tired and asked if I would take over the driving. I didn't know how to tell him that I didn't have a clue. Luckily, I had been watching him quite closely so I made a good job of changing gears, but as I drove on through the night, with him snoring beside me, it struck me that while I was doing well enough when it came to keeping the car on the road, I had absolutely no idea how to stop!

Fortunately, my friend woke up before we ended up going over the edge of a ravine. After that, I got behind the wheel of a car whenever I had the opportunity, and learned how to drive it.

Obviously, neither Pat nor I were allowed to talk about our work in any correspondence. All letters had to be written bearing in mind that they might be read by the censor before they reached their addressee. It wasn't just that we needed to keep military information secret; there had been quite a campaign asking people to keep bad news out of their letters to and from the front to keep morale high both at home and on the front line. American posters from the time encouraged people to write to the troops overseas. "Keep 'em smiling with letters from folks and friends". As a result, most of us willingly "self-censored", believing that keeping correspondence light and cheerful was as much a wartime duty as "make do and mend".

Dreams were still allowed, though. Pat and I often wrote about the world tour we'd take together when the war was over and speculated as to what work we might undertake when we were demobbed. All I knew was that, as much as I missed my family, I did not want to spend the rest of my life in England. I wanted to travel.

It's strange to think now that though Pat and I sometimes wrote to one another every day for weeks at a time and were closer to each other's affections than we had ever been, neither one of us knew what the other was doing when we put on our uniforms and went "into the office" for a shift. The Official Secrets Act applied between sisters too. I certainly couldn't tell Pat about Ratweek.

CHAPTER TWENTY-FIVE

Patricia

Back in England, in the September of 1944, things were changing rapidly for the Wrens of the Y Service. Paris had been liberated and Charles De Gaulle had formed a provisional government in France. The important French ports of Dieppe and Brest had fallen to the Allies. Allied troops had entered Belgium and freed the cities of Brussels, Antwerp, Ghent and Liège so that the Belgian government in exile was able to return from London. Luxembourg had been liberated. The Soviets were in Poland and Estonia and heading for Sofia in Bulgaria. Everywhere, the Germans were in retreat.

By the end of the month, the German garrison in Calais had surrendered. The twin terrors that were the Scharnhorst and the Gneisenau had both long since been neutralised. Once the Kriegsmarine capitulated, there was no longer any need for the Y stations, whose sole purpose had been listening to German naval traffic. Thus they were swiftly closed down. It wasn't long before my team at Abbot's Cliff was disbanded and we interceptors were drafted to other roles within the WRNS. I was sent up to London, to Admiralty, where I was set to work as a translator.

The Admiralty building in Whitehall was quite impressive. I remember walking into the entrance hall for the first time. There was a fireplace, with a fire burning in the grate. It was certainly a change from the direction-finding tower and I hoped it would prove to be a good place to spend the winter. I was taken to my new office and shown my desk and my first task. I was to translate a technical document describing the wiring of a U-boat.

I soon realised that, compared to listening in to German torpedo boats, translating U-boat manuals was laborious work indeed and I missed the excitement of a busy night at a Y station. But I had friends around me – several of my former Y station colleagues had been sent to Admiralty too – and I was billeted in a rather grand house on Chelsea Embankment that had been requisitioned for Wren accommodation. At least there was the London nightlife to enjoy. I looked forward to catching up with all that the city had to offer after being confined to Dover and Folkestone for so long. I went to the concerts at the National Gallery whenever I could. In many ways, though the war hadn't ended, it felt as though things were getting back to normal.

There was, however, still the threat of the V2s to deal with.

The V2s were the world's first long-range guided ballistic missiles. They were some 14 metres tall and were powered by a liquid propellant rocket engine. Launched vertically, they could reach hitherto unimaginable heights. Travelling at more than 3,500 mph and with a range of some 200 miles, they were the most sophisticated weapons the war had so far seen. They each carried a ton of explosives. The Germans may have been on the back foot across the Channel but the danger was far from over for those unfortunate British civilians within the V2s' reach.

The V2s were fired on London for the first time on 8 September 1944. That attack, which hit Chiswick, killed three and left 17 injured. It was at first reported as a gas explosion. This was perhaps an attempt to prevent the Germans knowing they had west London within their range. A later attack which hit the Woolworth's Store in New Cross killed 168, making it the most deadly single missile hit on British soil of the whole war. An attack on Smithfield's Market killed 110.

I had returned to the city right at the point at which the V2 attacks were at their most ferocious. Hundreds of V2s reached their targets, claiming some 2,724 lives in Britain alone. As well as London, they caused devastation in Essex, Norfolk and Luton. Though they were less accurate than the V1s had been, because the V2s travelled so much more quickly – faster than the speed of sound – they made no noise at all until they made impact. You simply couldn't see or hear them coming so there was no time to sound an air-raid siren or find a place of safety.

It would not be until 1945 that the Allies were able to capture all the V2 launch sites and bring this new danger to an end. For me, in the meantime, it was a case of always remembering to take my tin hat whenever I stepped outside.

CHAPTER TWENTY-SIX

Jean

While Pat was in Chelsea avoiding the V2s, I was still enjoying life in Puglia. However it was clear that there had been another shift in the war – the Allies had recently taken Rimini – and it might not be long until my role as a code and cipher officer was also surplus to requirements.

In our letters, Pat and I speculated as to how much longer it would be before I was able to come home. Several of the FANYs who had been in Italy alongside me had gone back to England already, to learn Japanese in preparation for being sent to the Far East. Our mother had put the kibosh on that idea as far as I was concerned. Still only 19, I was too young to go to a new overseas posting without her permission. I had to be 21 for that. So perhaps Pat and I would both be in London at the same time. Before then though, there were parts of Italy I still wanted to see.

Rome was a free city and in November 1944, I finally got to visit it. I marvelled at my luck in a letter to my sister.

"It does seem incredible. There's St Paul touring the Middle East for 20-odd years saying 'I must see Rome', and here's me saying 'can I have leave please' and going there. I hope it's an omen of things to come."

I visited Florence on the same trip. Strictly speaking, I wasn't supposed to be in Florence and I certainly wasn't supposed to have hitched to get there. Unlike Rome, Florence was still very close to the front line and you could hear firing in the Tuscan hills around her. I saw my first dead body in a ditch nearby.

I stayed for just one night in Florence. Everything but the magnificent Duomo was closed. By the time I got there, I had already seen St Peter's, but I found the Duomo, the Cathedral of Santa Maria Dei Fiori to give it its full name, far more impressive. It felt more spiritually fulfilling somehow. I had a conversation with a local man, the only other person in the nave that day, about the difference.

"In Rome you go to look around," he said. "In Florence you come to pray." I knew exactly what he meant.

I wrote to Pat when I got back to my base after that special trip. To make things even more special, we'd received news of our father right before I left Torre a Mare on leave. A letter had arrived at Newland Hall. Daddy couldn't say much but it was hugely comforting to have heard from him all the same. He told our mother that he was well, he was still singing and that the Japanese camp commandant seemed like a reasonable sort of man. All of which was encouraging.

C/Ens J Owtram FANY
Nr 2 SP Sigs Corp
CMF

28/11/44

My darlingest Patsy,

Well, I'm back home again. Florence and Rome are too perfect to be quite true. On the last night we walked down to the colosseum in the moonlight. I just cannot describe it, it was so vast and peaceful, but so full of ghosts. You could feel them all round you and it was completely quiet. St Peter's and the Sistine chapel and the Rafael rooms were so beautiful one can't even try! And I visited Keats and Shelley's graves and the house Keats died in. His stone doesn't say his name at all, just "a young English poet" and the epitaph, "Here lies one whose name was writ in water."

In the house is a letter from Severn describing his death. His very last words were "Thank God it has come at last." It was all so frustrated and tragic. I've seen Dante, Michelangelo,

Chapter Twenty-Six

Rafael, L. da Vinci, Galileo etc's graves. The most impressive
of all are the white crosses by the Florence road though.

Isn't it heaven about Daddy? I got Mummy's letters with
details last night. He must be OK if he's singing and donating
blood etc. Oh darling, isn't it the most wonderful relief and if the
Herr Commandant is really pro us there's a good chance of his
ultimate survival, which was beyond my wildest hopes by now.

A full-length sea-mail is in process of construction with
details of my leave. Your lovely beautiful card arrived in my
absence also delirious postcard assuring my inability to expire.
Bless you honey. Do take care of the nasty V2s and never
go out without a tin hat and chainmail. With all my love
sweetheart Jane xxxx

Around the same time, back in Torre a Mare I met someone
who broke through my resolve to avoid romantic entanglements
for the duration of the war. I mentioned him in a letter to Pat
just a few days later. I'd been visiting friends at a nearby
convalescent home, north of Bari. We FANYs often went there
to help raise the morale of the soldiers and airmen who'd been
sent there to recover. It was always good fun. The "convalescent
depot", as I called it, threw the most marvellous parties.

"My birthday was well and truly celebrated in the end. The night
before I went to a nice friendly dinner in Geoff's Mess, and Tommy
Matthias (RAF) got back from Cairo with loads of things I'd asked him

to buy me. So next day I lunched with him and got them. They include silk stockings, sandals, material for frocks and skirts, lipsticks etc etc. We joined a lot of his friends and had a cheerful lunch and four of us went to The Great Dictator *and I arranged to go to lunch again next day. Which some did and met a friend from Cairo, Robby, who joined the party, and we ate snacks for lunch and talked and drank intoxicating liquor and went up to their room and continued in a pleasant and casual manner, people drifting in and out as the mood took them. The party had grown to 14 regulars and various outpatients. So I had tea with a Naval boy and we listened to Mozart on his gramophone and more people arrived with more drink and Tommy's devastating cousin, a Wing Co. with a mention, aged 29.5, a honey, called Lewie, arrived too."*

Lewie, a much-decorated RAF wing commander, was soon to become a regular feature of my correspondence with my sister. Being in Italy was an adventure. Falling in love in Italy was something else again. At last I think I understood what all the fuss was about!

After all the progress the Allies had been making in France and in northern Italy, at one point I thought there might just be a chance I could be spending Christmas 1944 back at Newland Hall. It wasn't to happen. As Christmas drew near, I was still needed in Torre a Mare. It was to be the first time I had ever spent 25 December away from Lancashire and my family. As such, I hoped it would be special. My fellow FANYs and my friends from the other forces stationed nearby had plans to make it so.

On Christmas Eve afternoon we kicked off the festivities by singing carols around all the nearby messes. It was a glorified pub crawl really and some people got very merry indeed. Unfortunately, I was not able to join in with the drinking and the endless toasts, since I was going to be on duty at 2300 hours.

After the carol singing, we had a sumptuous dinner, in the style of a traditional Italian "vigilia di Natale" feast. It was very nice except that one of our number – Wally – was conspicuously absent from his place at the table. I took it upon myself to distract his best friend, Eric, from Wally's empty seat – they were usually like Tweedle Dum and Tweedle Dee – until it was time for me to go to work. It felt like hard luck to get the Christmas Eve night shift and miss the best of the party but at least it was a relatively quiet time to be working.

I described Christmas Day's festivities in a Boxing Day letter to Pat.

From C/Ens J. Owtram FANY
ME57
CMF

26th Dec 1944

My own darling Trish.

I wonder how Xmas day was kep' up in The Olde Home. With much hilarity and alcohol, I hope…

Three of us went to church at 0700 and then when we came off duty Jane and I went to the Club and saw her ex-fiancé and various other members of the same crowd, and all had breakfast and then five of us went to church which was lovely. We sang various carols and had the full morning service, not the Army Prayer Book abridged version which I've been to ever since I came out. Then we walked home (it was a glorious day) via the offices and I wished everyone happy Xmas, had lunch and then Jane and I slept till dinner time.

Dinner was marvellous: turkey, pork, pud, mince pies etc and lashings of drink including fizz. Then we all danced and played silly games till 2330 and then went up to the Allied Officers Club. We danced and drank some more till that closed too and then Tommy and Garry and a certain Lucas and ERIC and Jane and I and LEWIE (!) came back in Tommy's jeep and finished up in one of their many rooms telling shaggy dogs and singing etc and all rather alcoholic and fun.

But do you remember LEWIE? He was the Mark I heartthrob some weeks back and I hadn't seen him for ages (which had sent the HT bounding) and then last night there we were again! And he kissed me goodnight, tho' admittedly we were all a little happy by then. But still-! So the vibrations

are now rocking the Imperiale Albergo. You'd like him tho',
he really is a honey…"

But there was sad news too. That same letter to my sister
continued,

"The only shadow on the whole festa was that Eric's great friend
(and ours) Wally was missing the day before in an aircraft. I'd
been to a concert with the two of them (The Gruesome Twosome)
on Sat and Wally'd been going next day probably. So we said a
rather casual goodbye as one does, and next day the plane was
missing. On Xmas morning we heard that it had crashed and the
crew were killed and Wally had died when they got him out. He
was so young and so sweet, and he and Eric were inseparable.
So I spent my time looking after Eric who has been badly shaken
but of course won't show it, which is all rather pathetic. But it
does turn one's inside over a bit when friends get killed like that
doesn't it? And I was very fond of poor little Wally. Today is all
a bit miz as yet (I've just had breakfast with Eric, as we were
staying at the club last night) Lewie and Tommy have gone to
work and Garry and Jane are still asleep.

What an extremely egotistical air letter! Sorry. I am longing
to know what you did. I kept thinking of you, tho' not miserably
(except in the office) because there wasn't time and everyone was
so nice. Bless you my sweet, and take care of yourself.

With all my love,
Jane
Xxx

In the days that followed, I made a continued effort to take poor Eric's mind off the untimely loss of his best friend. Such losses were never easy to bear and somehow it being Christmas made it feel so much worse. We'd said "goodbye" to poor Wally so casually, never imagining for a moment that it might be the last time. But that was the reality of war. Whenever we forgot for a moment that our freedom was being paid for in lives all over Europe, we were given a sharp reminder. For all the spontaneous opera and sunshine and local wine that made being stationed in Italy so wonderful, we were not, in fact, on holiday. While the Yugoslav Partisans had made a lot of headway in the Balkans since Ratweek, the Germans were still in Kosovo and Bosnia. There was still work to be done. We were still at war.

CHAPTER TWENTY-SEVEN

Jean

As 1945 began, I was soon distracted by my own affairs again. At New Year it snowed. I was learning that the blissful Puglian summers could be matched by quite miserable winters, that were just as bad as January in Lancaster only without the benefit of being able to come home to hot water and a carpeted floor. The stone floor of the Villa Anna was lovely in the heat of July and August but in the winter it turned the place into a gigantic refrigerator. With cockroaches! The cockroaches must have been as cold as we humans were, since they always congregated by the fireplace.

All the same, I was in quite a good mood as I wrote to Pat on New Year's Day. Even if New Year's Eve in Bari hadn't gone exactly as planned.

"Happy New Year darling! Which doesn't seem such a farce as usual. I expect you and Mummy saw it in if you were still at home. I was at the

Allied Officers club singing Auld Lang Syne with millions of decidedly merry revellers totally unknown to me, all embracing each other fondly. Which combined with gin had a most depressing effect. Also Jane and I had got a date with the wrong party and the others were there and we were all completely miserable and browned off!!! But a terrific reconciliation followed – very dramatic and rather funny – afterwards and Jane and I spent the night on a ship because we couldn't get home, and it creaked and swayed just like The Boat Home (which is a catch phrase) so it was quite amusing really and the party was fun, however unfortunately composed. But I do think the New Year tends to depress one, don't you? Funny to think it's just a year since I was home on embarkation leave. Coo, that was an emotional New Year. It was almost the worst bit of saying goodbye. 'Where will we be in 12 months' time?' etc. That and seeing you off in London, sweet. A horrible sort of empty feeling as the train went out, and limitless expanses of empty platform. Thank goodness one can start thinking about trains coming in now!"

As I recalled the bittersweet experience of leaving England for the first time at the beginning of 1944, I was optimistic that I would be going home soon. And a couple of days later, Lewie was back in town, to turn my heart upside down. Unable to share my romantic tribulations with anyone in Torre a Mare, I poured my out my feelings to Pat.

"At present I'm at the outskirts of what may culminate in rather an emotional crisis! You probably recollect Lewie, my glamorous Wing Commander. I saw him yesterday while I was out with someone else and

as usual we all joined forces and went round to his mess. Subsequently I came home in the back of a 15-cwt truck with Lewie and oh my! I thought he'd never been conscious of my existence but he is – ! Oh Patsy, I wish I knew just what I wanted, but as I have the faintest doubts I suppose this can't be it! Anyway, he hasn't asked me yet, but I've never been so happy as last night after we'd said goodnight and I'd stopped being all took aback and breathless and so on. Because you see Lewie is very quiet and quite unemotional as a rule, and I certainly wasn't expecting anything at all. But don't worry, I shouldn't do anything before I got home anyway, because this is such an unreal atmosphere one is hardly ever myself (I wasn't last night I know!) and one couldn't build one's future on this sort of basis. But it's all very thoughtful making.

Anyway, we hardly know each other, and at this rate never shall! But I'm going on the assumption that if he wants to see me again he will, and if not I'm not going chasing after him all round town. But I do wish he'd contact me! He's doing a parachute course at present (they don't teach RAF to jump in the normal way so that they're less eager to bale out!!) and he's promised I shall see him do his first jump so I'm hoping he'll remember.

I'll write you a real letter soon I promise, but this is the degenerate garbling of a love-sick loon. Oh coo! If this is what they make all the fuss about they're dead right. But I've always been just miserable before, never quite so ecstatic as at present!

I wish I wasn't quite so young, I know lots of people engaged at 19 but I don't think it's very wise – until it comes to me! Anyway, this is purely hypothetical, I expect Lewie is engaged or a misogynist (?) or misanthrope or whatever you call them. Sweet, if I don't stop drivelling I'll explode with wanting to see him and you.

So goodnight my own honey sister and God bless.
With all my love.
Jane

Having decided that the elusive Lewie might actually be interested in me, I could have howled when a couple of days later I was sent from Torre a Mare to a posting further along the coast at Monopoli without being able to tell him where I was going! I did get the news to Lewie eventually, but alas the romance did not last long in any case. Lewie wasn't a misogynist but by the end of the spring, I had discovered that he was indeed engaged to be married. He had a fiancée in Algiers.

Thankfully, there were plenty of distractions to take my mind off my bruised heart. I was moved from Monopoli back to Torre a Mare. By March, the staff in my office had shrunk from eight to two. We no longer had to work night shifts and there were plenty of parties as more and more people were called back to Britain and wanted a big send-off. Someone in the officer's mess adopted a stray puppy which we took turns to walk. Things picked up to the point that sometimes I wished my time in Italy wouldn't come to an end after all, as this letter shows.

Chapter Twenty-Seven

From C/Ens J. Owtram F.A.N.Y.
Nr. 2. S.P. Sigs. Coy.
C.M.F.

8th April 45

My darling Trix,

I'm sure the 8th April is someone's birthday or something but I can't remember what. However I haven't had any mail for ages as it's all going in different directions. Doubtless it'll all catch me up one day. I wrote to Daddy on 5th as per instructions. Isn't it difficult to compress anything into 25 words and not sound formal and stilted?

Life is very good indeed at present, I wish I wasn't going. We sit in the lounge at nights and talk, or rather Tony and Althea talk and we listen. Last night only we three were in so it was rather like being at home with Althea mending stockings and the puppy falling off chairs, and the fire and just talking as one chose. Very peaceful. Tony knows Moray and Arisaig well so we got deep into those and I could have howled. He likes it as much as I do, and it was heaven to talk about all the bits we knew. Doesn't it all seem ages ago? I do so hope things like that will come back someday.

The other day the Town Mayor came round to the mess and asked for two volunteers to search Italian women for things they were supposed to be stealing. So as there was no one else in another Jean (Heller) and I said OK and we had to make these ruddy women undress completely in case they'd hidden things under their clothes! It was so sordid and dreary I felt literally sick. But my goodness, the jobs they find for one in the army!

At present there are just us three girls – Jean, Althea and Me – and the three men – Arthur Burton, Tony Woodhouse and Harry Bennett – in the mess. Which is great fun and so much nicer than gaggles of FANYs. And Tony is a marvellous talker and Arthur and I fool around infantilely and Harry is much older and reminds me of a hypothetical grandfather (we talk about Bezique and billiards). Althea is Tony's secretary and very amusing and kind and nice. I've laughed more in the last week than since I left home I think!

What does Lilly think about the news about Vienna? They're bound to do an awful lot of damage if it's really in a state of siege, I suppose, but the Russians seem to be right inside already. By the time you get this it'll have fallen I imagine.

Tonight there are supposed to be "traditional religious processions" with fireworks at 1730 according to Port orders. So we are going to go and watch! I've no idea what the festa is about, first Sunday after Easter means nothing to me. It's probably St Whatsit the Obscure. I always felt so sorry for him, it was such a dreary little St Jude wasn't it? Not inspiring. St Jean the Inconspicuous now, that would be madly exciting for *posterity. Oh dear, what drivel. But I do wonder who attached all these little labels to quite harmless saints. Honey, I am so longing to see you again. There'll be such a fantastic number of things to talk about too. Marvellous. Let's share a room and then we can talk all night. Bless you honey.*

All my love.
Jane

By the time Pat got my letter, Vienna had indeed fallen. The Germans were in retreat across Austria with the Soviets in hot pursuit. Alas, in the wake of the fleeing Germans, an orgy of looting and violence ensued – both by the second wave of Soviet soldiers and even by desperate Austrians who saw a chance to enrich themselves at their neighbours' expense. The lawlessness and debauchery left Vienna and her people in ruins. Reading all about it in *The Union Jack*, I felt great sadness for Lilly and Edith and the beautiful, cultured city they'd carried in their hearts all this time. The city I had loved in my imagination.

CHAPTER TWENTY-EIGHT

Patricia

Spring 1945

I was very glad indeed when I was transferred from Admiralty to SHAEF, the Supreme Headquarters of the Allied Expeditionary Force.

SHAEF was under the command of U.S. General Dwight D. Eisenhower and the intelligence department where I worked, which was situated on the top floor of Peter Robinson, a department store at Oxford Circus (which is now TopShop), was staffed by German-speaking American and British servicemen and women.

This time I was given a research role. I was to read through files retrieved from the Gau Baden-Elsass, the Nazi administrative district encompassing the German state of Baden and occupied Alsace. The *Gau* – which simply means "region" – was controlled by a *Gauleiter* or regional leader, called Robert Wagner. The gauleiter had a significant amount of power regarding the local administration of propaganda and surveillance.

For the most part the papers I dealt with documented the conduct of ordinary people as seen through the eyes of the *Zellenleiter*. The zellenleiter were low-level domestic spies, Nazi party members, who were paid to snoop on their neighbours' "unpatriotic" acts. My job was to sift through their reports and other official documents for evidence of possible war crimes (as a result of his activities, Robert Wagner would be executed in Strasbourg in 1946).

I was struck but not entirely surprised by the zeal with which some of the zellenleiter and blockleiter had carried out their low-level spying work. I remember finding amongst the paperwork a photograph of a newly graduated group of low-grade German line crossing agents posing proudly in rows for the camera, after completing their training as spies. I couldn't help thinking that the fact that the photo existed at all summed up why Germany's wartime intelligence was not all that it might have been. *Look! Here are our secret agents!* It made an extraordinary contrast to the discretion and secrecy with which we Y Service Wrens had been expected to conduct ourselves.

Though it was slightly more interesting than translating U-boat manuals, working on the Gau Baden-Elsass papers was still less dramatic than the 24/7 intensity of the Y stations and I began to wonder whether being a Wren was all it was cracked up to be. I'd spent two years right at the heart of things. Was this glorified secretarial work to be my future now?

I had passed two boards for a WRNS commission – one of which took place in a basement during an air raid. My interviewer and I sat opposite one another on packing cases with a storm lantern for light – and I knew that my promotion was being delayed simply because my German language skills were needed in Y and now for this work. Indeed, Freddie Marshall later wrote, "personnel serving in intelligence were often denied the prospect of promotion that would have been available in other branches or categories. This was certainly the case in Special Duties, for many, if not most, of these Wrens were officer material and WRNS headquarters were so eager to have their services in other categories that for a time it was necessary to place a ban on Special Duties officers transferring to other categories."

The only consolation was that working with the Americans in what was effectively an American base meant I got access to PX rations. The PX, which stood for Post Exchange, was the American version of the NAAFI (The Navy, Army and Air Force Institutes) stores found on British military bases. At the PX, we could get all sorts of American goodies such as Camel cigarettes and Hershey's chocolate bars, which I sent to Bob at school – the sweets, not the cigarettes. There seemed to be no restrictions on how much you could buy. You could take a suitcase and load it up if you wanted to. Some did. We were even able to get nylons from time to time. It was quite a privilege after years of rationing. I became a big fan of peanut butter sandwiches, which I tried for the first time ever in the SHAEF canteen.

I was at SHAEF during the early months of 1945, as the Allied troops pushed on into Germany and Eastern Europe and more disturbing documents reached our offices from the front line. The zellenleiter files started to seem very petty indeed as the photographs and reports from the concentration camps such as Auschwitz and Dachau started to cross the desks of some of my colleagues. We were deeply shocked but because of our pledge of secrecy we could not mention them outside the office.

However, General Eisenhower thought it was very important to take photographs of the camps as they were liberated. Later he would say of his own visits to the camps in April 1945, "I felt it my duty to be in a position from then on to testify at first hand about these things in case there ever grew up at home the belief or assumption that 'the stories of Nazi brutality were just propaganda'... I sent communications to both Washington and London, urging the two governments to send instantly to Germany a random group of newspaper editors and representative groups from the national legislatures. I felt that the evidence should be immediately placed before the American and British publics in a fashion that would leave no room for cynical doubt."

I hoped that General Eisenhower's good intentions weren't in vain. From the top floor of the bus my way to work, I saw a queue of people waiting outside the wax museum at 60 Oxford Street, a sort of bargain basement Madame Tussaud's, where an enterprising businessman had staged an exhibition called "The War In Wax: The Horrors of the German concentration camps all in life-like and life-size figures."

That exhibition actually opened in January 1945, months before Auschwitz was liberated and while the V2s were still falling on London. It cost 6d to see it. I wondered about the emotions of both the exhibitor and the people in the queue.

CHAPTER TWENTY-NINE

Jean

Life in Italy continued at a relatively gentle pace. More and more people returned to the UK, leaving the signal office at Torre a Mare with a skeleton staff. As one of the few remaining code and cipher officers, I was given a promotion and found myself head of my shift.

There was a definite sense that things were winding down so it was quite a shock when on 9 April 1945, Bari was rocked by a huge explosion. Everyone's first thought was that Bari was under enemy attack, just as it had been in December 1943, when the Luftwaffe had attacked ships in the harbour, exploding the US Liberty Ship John Harvey with its secret cargo of 2,000 mustard-gas-filled bombs. The truth of the matter this time was more prosaic, if no less tragic.

It happened as the SS Charles Henderson, another US Liberty ship, which had taken part in the D-Day landings, was being unloaded. The Charles Henderson was carrying munitions, including a number of 1,000lb and 500lb demolition bombs. It was berthed right in the middle of the harbour and only half the ship's cargo had been moved onto the dockside when one of the bombs still onboard was accidentally detonated. The resulting explosion devastated buildings all along the waterfront. Seven ships were destroyed, including the SS Lucia C, which was carrying a cargo of petrol that promptly burst into flame and became a huge conflagration. More than 500 were killed, including every member of the SS Charles Henderson's crew except for the chief engineer, who had gone ashore. More than 1,800 were injured.

It's believed that the accident was caused because the Charles Henderson's cargo was being unloaded at haste and without proper safety precautions, as the crew doing the offloading was being paid by the unit. The faster they worked, the more they could earn.

When I heard what had happened and saw how the incident was being reported in the British press, I wrote home in an exercise of damage limitation.

"My darling Mummy,

Thank you so much for your air letter. I do hope you've heard by now that I am very much in the land of the living. I didn't cable as someone told me letters were just as quick nowadays.

We haven't much glass left in town certainly, but the casualties weren't nearly as heavy as they expected. I never heard a thing being 20 or 30 miles away at the time…"

I sent Pat a slightly more descriptive version of the same events.

"As regards the Big Bang let me assure you once more I was not rpt not promenading the docks then or after so I haven't even seen the chaos I understand the papers informed you reigned supreme. Actually you'd hardly notice it now; the windows are back and the roads are repaired and the ship that got burnt out is floating again. It looked rather lovely several nights after while it was still turning, red hot down to the water line at one end ('Ball of fire' not to be taken too literally being the current equivalent of 'just the job')…"

Having reassured both Pat and my mother that all was well, I continued in my usual upbeat manner in the spirit of keeping calm and carrying on. Lewie the airman was a distant memory but I'd allowed a friend to read my palm in the hope of better romantic news.

"My romantic horizon is likewise devoid of ships (?) at the moment. Unfortunately, the people who really do seem ideal are invariably too happily so. It really is sickening!… The trouble

is, the people who want to get married are always (so I'm told) the ones who finish as governesses to other people's children. According to my hand I shall have a legitimate child and one illegitimate one – rather intriguing and, one trusts, indicated a happy married life. Which would be so pleasantly restful. However, I have a strong career line too, to my horror. I do dislike Women With A Purpose. More on another card."

I would come to think differently about "women with a purpose" in my later years but in the spring of 1945, I was still very young and impressionable. I continued my letter as promised on another card.

From c/Ens J Owtram FANY

Nr 2 SP Sigs Corp

CMF

28th Apr 45

Part 2

I think I finished answering your questions in Part 1 so I'll cover the last week's social whirl in this one. Which must be madly boring for you on second thought, being very similar week by week. Still last time was a bit different as Eric picked me up for lunch at our local black market café where we sat in the sun and ate spaghetti and omelettes and drank sun-warmed vino (just like drinking liquid silk) and then we went down to the grotto downstairs and looked at the sea (green like bath salts) and talked about the war and then I had a driving lesson in the jeep over cart tracks and then back down the main road. We had tea in town at 6 and stayed at the club talking till 8 and had dinner and drank tomato juice – frightfully unalcoholic altogether and half way through dinner I recalled your account of dining with Godfrey and talking cotton because I found I was doing precisely the same! We talked farming and cotton all evening solidly! And it was most entertaining. When we went up to dance they were playing Paper Doll and after that the evening couldn't miss. I've never seen the club so cheerful and sober and really lovely. I had the most celestial evening ever and Eric felt just the same.

The band played beautifully and really enjoyed themselves and there was a very nice crowd there all with the party spirit and everything just swam along. It was fun. Then when we got back about 1, we decided to go and look at the Trulli houses in the moonlight (the ones like this – drawing) so we dashed off 66 miles there and back and they looked perfect. (Did you know you could see colours in moonlight? I didn't before). And we sat on top of the hills and talked about fishing in Scotland. We got home about 3.30 eventually. Eric is a dear. It's all rather fun and unromantic. I love going out with him, it's no effort! But it is odd how wherever I am I always seem to be arguing about a) cotton b) farming c) sending innocent young things overseas and d) marriage. I'm going to write to Grandboff and get the low down on the Milk marketing board etc I think so that I have something to support my arguments! Did I mention Jane and I are going on leave to Sorrento and Rome next week? It should be fun. All my love sweetie pie.

Jane

It seems that 28 April 1945 was a good day for me but it turned into a very bad one for Benito Mussolini, Il Duce.

The former Italian dictator was trying to flee to Switzerland, disguised in the uniform of a German airman, when he was captured by Italian partisans near Lake Como. Mussolini and his mistress, Carla Petacci, were executed by machine gun and their bodies were taken to Milan, to be displayed in the Piazzale Loreto, where less than a year before the SS had displayed the bodies of 15 executed partisans. Of course we soon heard all about it in Torre a Mare. Mussolini and Petacci were strung up by their feet by the angry crowds. Thousands came to see the corpse of the man who had allied Italy to the Nazis in 1936 and consigned his nation to the wrong side of the war.

CHAPTER THIRTY

Patricia

All the while, the Allied forces were inching closer to a final victory in Europe. By now, the Allies had taken more than 1,500,000 Axis prisoners on the Western Front and Hitler was cornered in his bunker in Berlin. On 30 April, two days after the death of his former ally Mussolini, he took his own life by swallowing a cyanide capsule before shooting himself in the head. He took his new wife, Eva Braun, whom he had married just the day before, with him. His demise was announced by German radio on 1 May. It was described as an "heroic" death.

Hitler had left instructions that he was to be succeeded at the head of the Reich by Grand Admiral Karl Dönitz with Joseph Goebbels, Hitler's minister of propaganda, as second-in-command. Goebbels took his own life a day after Hitler (having instructed his wife to kill their six children first). Dönitz vowed in his inaugural speech to the shattered German nation that he would fight on but Heinrich Himmler had already made secret overtures towards the Allies in pursuit of peace and Dönitz too would soon be busily negotiating an end to war that would keep as much of Germany as possible out of Soviet occupation.

On 2 May, the remaining German forces in Italy surrendered. That same day the Battle of Berlin concluded with German surrender there. On 4 May, Field Marshall Montgomery, Monty, accepted the surrender of German forces in north-west Germany, the Netherlands and Denmark. A day later, the Kriegsmarine was told to stand down the last of the U-boats. On 6 May, Hermann Göring, the highest-ranking Nazi still alive, surrendered to US Forces at the Germany-Austria border. Then on 7 May, the German General Alfred Jodl signed the unconditional surrender on behalf of the German High Command at the SHAEF headquarters in Reims, northern France.

The news of the unconditional surrender broke late that same evening. It didn't come as a surprise to me exactly, but it still took a while for the idea that the war in Europe was finally truly over to sink in. A radio news bulletin and the last editions of 7 May newspapers announced that the following day, 8 May, would be a national holiday, which thenceforth would be known as Victory in Europe, or VE Day.

The government had been preparing for a big celebration for a while already and in the early hours of 8 May, Winston Churchill himself made sure that the Ministry of Food could guarantee beer supplies for London. As the news spread, some people started celebrating early in London's pubs and bars. Overnight, the streets were festooned with Union flags and red, white and blue bunting.

By lunchtime the next day, everyone was ready for a party. London's streets were closed so that neighbours could bring out their tables and chairs and eat together. The centre of the city was full of people singing, dancing and laughing, and making the most of those all-important beer supplies.

At 3pm, Winston Churchill addressed the nation in a radio broadcast that was cheering but cautious. It was a wonderful moment, like a collective exhalation at the end of a long period when we'd all been holding our breath, though I was very glad to hear him remind his listeners that the war in the Far East and the Pacific was not yet won.

The King also made a radio broadcast that day, recognising that while the nation was celebrating, we should not forget those who had made the ultimate sacrifice for this happy victory. He told us, "There is great comfort in the thought that the years of darkness and danger in which the children of our country have grown up are over and, please God, forever. We shall have failed and the blood of our dearest will have flowed in vain if the victory which they died to win does not lead to a lasting peace, founded on justice and good will.

"To that, then, let us turn our thoughts to this day of just triumph and proud sorrow, and then take up our work again, resolved as a people to do nothing unworthy of those who died for us, and to make the world such a world as they would have desired for their children and for ours."

With a group of friends from SHAEF and the Wrens, I joined the throng heading down to the Mall to see the Royal Family come out onto the balcony of Buckingham Palace. As hundreds of thousands of people continued to gather throughout the day, they had to make a total of eight balcony appearances to be sure that everyone who turned up had the chance of a seeing a royal wave. On our way there, we saw Mountbatten being whisked in a car.

I cheered and waved as loudly as anyone as I saw the King and Queen step out to greet us with the Princesses, Elizabeth and Margaret, beside them. The Queen and Princess Margaret wore pale green. Princess Elizabeth proudly wore her ATS uniform. They flanked Winston Churchill, the man of the hour.

Later, the King and Queen made a last balcony appearance without the Princesses, who had been allowed to join the crowds below, enjoying their anonymity as they revelled in the joyful atmosphere with the rest of us. It was a moment when the usual conventions were swept aside and rank and social privilege didn't matter. A princess could dance with a porter that night.

From Buckingham Palace, I joined friends for a raucous dinner at a nearby services club. The party went on into the early hours of 9 May. Piccadilly Circus was heaving with revellers. People jumped into the fountains in Trafalgar Square. There were bonfires and fireworks all over the city. The pubs stayed open until their taps ran dry. Naturally there was a certain amount of bad behaviour. I was somewhat taken aback by the number of street-walkers who seemed to be targeting any man in uniform that day.

I was in a contemplative mood as I walked back to the Wrens' house in Chelsea. Of course VE Day was a day of huge jubilation for everyone who'd been on our side of the war but it was tinged with more than a little sadness for our family. As Churchill had rightly reminded the nation, the Germans may have surrendered but the Japanese fought on. It wouldn't be until VJ – for "Victory in Japan" – Day, that the Owtrams could truly celebrate.

In her diary, under 8 May, our mother wrote: "*VE Day… PM Broadcast at 3. Pops, Bob, Lilly and I to Thanksgiving Service at 7.0. Church full… Please God it will be VJ Day and darling Cary home.*"

I know that Jean and I were thinking exactly the same thing. VE Day was not the end for us by any means, but it was nonetheless a moment of great hope. Now that the Allied Forces were no longer fighting the Germans, they could concentrate their full efforts on the Japanese and, surely, bring our personal anxiety to a swift and happy conclusion.

CHAPTER THIRTY-ONE

Jean

C/Ens J. Owtram. F.A.N.Y.

Nr. 2 S.P. Signals Company

CMF

VE Day (8.5.45)

My double darling Patsy,

Isn't this just so wonderful and overwhelming. One knew it was on its way but now it just leaves me feeling mentally exhausted. I wish I had been in London, it must have been colossal. Were you in the crowd outside Buck House? We heard a recording of that. And did you have a riotous dinner at Pruniers? Oh honey, it is glorious, isn't it? No more organised murder in all of Europe. Lots of the people here are just blasé and unexcited. I can't understand it. Even if it doesn't affect them personally or if millions of people are still starving or there is another war to be finished it's just wonderful for the men who have been fighting all this time and for the people who've been in concentration camps and POW camps for all these years.

We were up at the Allied Officers Club when the news came through on Monday night. They brought round copies of the Union Jack's special edition and there was a poster up on the wall saying "Germany: the end. Peace in Europe." No one started breaking the place up or anything. We read the paper as we danced and everyone looked a bit dazed, and you could feel the excitement and relief all over the room. Yesterday Eric took me down to Taranto to have lunch in his old mess and we all listened to Churchill in the mess's canteen. When we got upstairs afterwards every ship in the port was sounding its siren and all the flags were out and people were letting off revolvers into the air all round. It was very impressive. As usual I wanted to cry! In the evening I was on duty so we heard the King's broadcast in the office. Also the programmes before and after.

Oh honey, this is all so dramatic and happy and wonderful. It's almost worth the five and a hald years before. And Churchill's message to the Far East too was so hopeful – "Lift up your hearts for we are coming". I wish I was at home just for these few days. It's very thrilling being out here but I'd love to be with you all. Still, it won't be so long now, probably three or four months they say. Now the entire camp is taking over all the fishing boats in the harbour so I must away and join them!

Bless you honey, and have a wild and woolly VE Day (we've all got CB for six days!!! Why heaven only knows, but I don't intend to keep it too vigorously). All my love my sweetest,

Jane
XXX

I heard the news that the Germans had surrendered on the evening of 7 of May. We already knew that the last of the Germans in Italy had given up the fight and that Berlin had rolled over too, but we didn't expect the final surrender to happen quite so quickly. The Nazi high command would surely fight to the bitter end. But at last the end had come. For Europe at least.

As it happened, I was very lucky that I wasn't in Torre a Mare when the news of Germany's final surrender came through, because it meant that I got to see some of the celebrations in Taranto. I had a wonderful time. Upon getting back to Torre, I asked my fellow FANYs how they had marked the occasion. My question was met with a slightly sour response. They'd had to work through all the excitement. The timing of my leave had been fortunate indeed.

All other leave was cancelled for the next few days and we were confined to barracks (CB). The powers that be were concerned that now there was no danger that Italy would fall back under Axis control, the Italians might turn against the Allies. In the event, there was no trouble at all, at least not where I was. We carried on as before, manning the office as usual.

Like Pat, I knew that Victory in Europe was only the *beginning* of the end for our family and while I was thrilled that the fight was over in Italy, the war was far from finished for Daddy. The real celebrations could begin when he was home.

> *C/Ens J Owtram FANY*
> *Nr 2 SP Signals Company CMF*
> *8th May 1945*

My darling Mummy,

It's just so wonderful I can hardly believe it. I just wish we could all be together for today, but the real "V" day for us will be when the other war is ended too. Please Heaven that won't be long to wait. I know you will be happy today for all the thousands of people for whom this is the end, but there is a sadness behind it because it doesn't bring Daddy back yet. But in due time this V-Day will shorten the other war, of course. Darling, God bless you and may you not have much longer to wait…

…with fondest love.
Your loving Jinks
xxxxx

CHAPTER THIRTY-TWO

Jean

Back when war was declared in 1939, I had imagined, as any 14-year-old girl might, that I was about to be plunged into a world of exciting danger in which the prospect of sudden death lurked around every corner. As it happened, the closest I came to death during my time as a FANY was in an incident that came shortly after VE Day.

Having spent six days confined to barracks, I was able to take the leave I'd been due earlier in the month. I travelled to Naples and Sorrento. From Sorrento, I sent a postcard and a box of beautiful local lemons back to Lancashire, wondering as I did so whether they would get there before I did.

I spent a beautiful afternoon playing tennis with some friends on a bluff overlooking the sea. We had finished playing and I was admiring the view when I saw some friends heading out from shore on a motor boat. I immediately jumped up onto a small hillock and waved and shouted to attract their attention. Alas, I was a little too vigorous in my waving and I lost my balance. I fell off the hillock and plunged straight over the cliff.

"Well, I suppose that's me done," I thought to myself as I plummeted towards the sea at breakneck speed. My friends at the top of the cliff and in the boat out in the bay thought the same. They all closed their eyes tightly and waited for the impact. The cliff led straight down to rocks. I was a goner for sure. What a silly, if spectacular, way to go.

But of course, as you know because you're reading this, I didn't fall to my death that day after all. By pure chance, I landed in the water rather than on the rocks and I came up spluttering with laughter.

My friends hauled me onto their boat and took me to the shore. They checked me over but I assured them that I was perfectly fine. Wet and a little surprised, but fine. They took my word for it.

I had to let Pat know, of course.

c/Ens J Owtram FANY at YWCA Sorrento. Italy.

22.5.45

My own honey bunch. Behold me returned from somewhere in the vicinity of Lethe, rescued from a watery end by a representative of Charon. And so on. To revert, I've been spending most of my time here up at the convalescent home which contains some of the nicest people I've ever met. Fun. So yesterday I went to play tennis which we did in the middle of the afternoon at a temperature never reached by Aga cooker. Consequently, when we saw the Con. Depot yacht sailing by just 30 feet beneath us it looked very pleasant and I thought it would be a good thing to have a lift. The S. African padre who had been playing said something vague about steps down the cliff, so I leapt blithely onto the wall and instantly lost my balance. Four or five feet down there was, by the way of all the deities on Olympus, a ledge covered with flowers. All the rest of the cliff was sheer jagged rock. So I turned a complete somersault on the ledge and took off again and did it take ages to hit the water!

Fortunately I missed the boat and they hauled me on board when I surfaced. But a couple of feet left or right on this cliff and this scrawl would not not not have reached you. So I'm a trifle dithery still, tho' frightfully hearty what-ho! On the boat etc! But then I was rescued by an MC who I'd rather adulated from a distance and who "admired my calm courage"! Whoopee! And subsequently was treated with respect and incredulity, I was teased mercilessly by everyone, which was fun. So after tea, when my things were dryish again, we returned to the court and played three sets straight off which meant missing dinner, so we four came down here and had eggs and chips and vino in a ristorante and then three of us went on to another molto nero marche one (black market in case that's illegible) and got appallingly tight on vermouth. Really, never have I been on such a bend. But one of the other two was an ultra-charming being called John who shoots and fishes etc and we got more and more nostalgic and sentimental talking about pheasant and grouse and rivers and woods and so on. Also he has beautiful manners and pours the top of a bottle into his own glass first, and always opens doors and so on, and as everyone is getting so casual now it is fun to be treated like porcelain. But to-day I feel just as if I'd been playing ball with a steam roller. Every little bit of me aches or is stiff or bumped!! Never again. Incidentally, I'm not repeating to Mama or she'll visualise me falling off all the cliffs in Italy. Quelle letter egotistique (?)! Maleesh. Tons and tons of love, your shattered Jane.

Later that same day, I joined my friends at a party. At first, everything seemed perfectly fine but at one point in the evening I began to shake so violently I thought I might shake all my teeth out. The shock of the fall had hit me at last. My friends quickly found a nurse who looked after me until I started to feel calmer again. She was extremely kind to me. While we sat together until I felt quite strong again, I told her about my family and how much I longed to go home now. After Italy, she was on her way to the Far East, she said.

A couple of days later, I heard news about my return to England. My departure was scheduled for the end of June. When I got back, I would get two weeks' leave, during which time I hoped to find a job so that when I was demobbed from the FANY I would not be conscripted to work in a factory.

Italy was at its best as spring turned into early summer. The Apennines were covered in dog roses and yellow broom – *ginestra* as the Italians call it – which scented the balmy warm air. The sea was perfect for swimming. It was all so lovely again. But one by one my friends had been moved on to other postings, leaving me a little lost and lonely as I held the fort without them.

However before I left, there was one last message for me to code. I was the senior officer on night duty now. There was so little to do that I told my juniors to "take a doss", leaving me in the office alone. I occupied myself with some tidying up and some administrative work. When the phone rang at three in the morning I leapt to take the call, hoping it would be something interesting.

The call was coming from the office of Fitzroy Maclean, Tito's liaison. I took down the instructions but the message I was to encode and have my team send to all concerned parties seemed ridiculous to me. All local leave for military personnel near Trieste was to be cancelled so that they would be available to take part in a cricket match.

A cricket match? How on earth could a cricket match be so important that it justified cancelling everyone's leave? I felt most disgruntled as I called my juniors back into the office and we passed the message on.

A few weeks later, I returned to England from Naples by sea, on a troop ship called The Duchess of Richmond. It was no luxury cruise ship, such as the one I had taken to Alexandria, but it was a jolly journey all the same. I was very glad to be going home at last.

CHAPTER THIRTY-THREE

Patricia

Since the summer of 1944 American heavy bomber aircraft, based on captured Pacific islands, had been able to strike directly at the Japanese mainland. By the summer of 1945 such raids had destroyed large areas of Japan's major cities and caused enormous casualties.

Then, on 6 August 1945, the US hit the Japanese city of Hiroshima with an atomic bomb known as "Little Boy". The bomb's blast, fire and radiation effects would ultimately kill more than 100,000 people.

The bombing of Hiroshima plunged the Japanese government and military into turmoil. The Americans had shown that they able to destroy a whole city with a single nuclear missile. Meanwhile, the Soviets were closing in too. They had moved into Manchuria and declared war on Japan on 9 August. On that same day the Americans detonated the atomic bomb they called "Fat Man" over Nagasaki, killing a further 80,000.

Less than a week later, Emperor Hirohito announced Japan's surrender to the Allies.

When she heard the news, our mother wrote in her diary:

Wednesday 15th August 1945

PEACE!! Japan has signed. POW are to be collected and flown home where possible. Heard it on 7 news this morning but it was also at 12 last night.

I could hardly believe it. After so long waiting and longing for our father to come home, my wish had come true. On 15 August, I again joined the crowds on the Mall, surging towards Buckingham Palace where, just as on VE Day, the Royal Family – the King, the Queen and the two princesses – came out onto the balcony to share our joy. The King gave a speech, which was broadcast over the radio, to mark the moment. He said, "Three months have passed since I asked you to join with me in an act of thanksgiving for the defeat of Germany.

"We then rejoiced that peace had returned to Europe, but we knew that a strong and relentless enemy still remained to be conquered in Asia. None could then tell how long or how heavy would prove the struggle that still awaited us.

"Japan has surrendered, so let us join in thanking Almighty God that war has ended throughout the world, and that in every country men may now turn their industry, skill, and science to repairing its frightful devastation and to building prosperity and happiness.

"Our sense of deliverance is overpowering, and with it all, we have a right to feel that we have done our duty.

"I ask you again at this solemn hour to remember all who have laid down their lives, and all who have endured the loss of those they love. Remember, too, the sufferings of those who fell into the hands of the enemy, whether as prisoners of war or because their homes had been overrun. They have been in our thoughts all through these dark years, and let us pray that one result of the defeat of Japan may be many happy reunions of those who have been long separated from each other."

The official "instrument of surrender" document was signed on board the USS Missouri in Tokyo Bay on 2 September. Before that happened, Admiral Lord Louis Mountbatten set into action Operation Tiderace and Operation Zipper, to liberate Singapore and Malaya respectively. Penang surrendered without resistance. Mountbatten was not expecting much of a battle in Singapore either, since the Japanese commander, General Itagaki Seishiro, had already agreed to stand by Hirohito's decision to end the fighting. All the same, after a farewell sake party at Singapore's famous Raffles hotel, 300 Japanese officers fell onto their swords, in the ancient practice of seppuku or hara-kiri, rather than be taken prisoner.

Mountbatten accepted the Japanese surrender in Singapore on 12 September 1945. With it came the end of the Japanese occupation of southeast Asia.

Suddenly, everything was quite different. At last we dared to anticipate seeing our father again.

While I was working at SHAEF, a list was sent around the office asking people to sign up if they were proficient in German shorthand. Not knowing why German shorthand might be important, I signed up. I later discovered that SHAEF had been looking for people who might be suitable to work as translators at the Nuremberg trials. Though I might have been able to do the work, it had come at the wrong time for me. In the light of my father's imminent return, my mother wanted the whole family to stay close by so that we could all be there for the day itself. Jean was back in England by now too. I agreed to our mother's request. Of course I wanted to be there when my father came home. Indeed it wasn't long before we heard that he was on his way. After such a long time of not knowing whether he was still alive, our hearts were full of happiness.

After three years of having our mail to him returned stamped "addressee missing", we knew he would receive our letters again. I wrote to him at once.

Chapter Thirty-Three

W.R.N.S. Quarters,
7 Chelsea Embankment
London SW3
18.9.45

My darling Daddy,

It is so lovely to think that when you get this you will be safe home in England again. Darling, how lovely it will be to see you… Oh darling it will be heaven. I have just seen the lovely cheerful airletter you wrote Mama before you started back, and of course she has sent a constant series of telegrams about every item of news. I wonder if it is really too late for you and her to have a third honeymoon in Scotland after you have had some leave at Newland. I think the family financial situation is very good! It had better be.

I can lay on some leave as soon as I know you have arrived, if that would be a good idea, and no doubt Jinks and Robert can too. Oh darling Dadda, it's so lovely to be able to think about these things! We are so excited. We will have to have millions of celebration parties. Hooray!

Tons of love darling. We are just so longing to see you –
All my love
Trish

CHAPTER THIRTY-FOUR

Jean

Of course the end of the war was what we had all longed for but now that I was back in England, I began to wonder what I would do next. I had been offered the opportunity to go to India with the FANY but, like Pat, I had come under gentle pressure from our mother to be at home for our father's return. He'd been in a prisoner of war camp for three years. How could we refuse to be there to greet him when he finally came home?

So I turned down India but I was concerned as to what might come next. With the FANY being disbanded, there was a danger that I could get called up by one of the other forces. I didn't want to end up in a munitions factory. I did not want to join the ATS. Nor did I ultimately want to spend the rest of my life in England. To fill time, I went back to London, where I lodged with a relative, and took a job with Ibbs and Tillett, an agency based on Wigmore Street near the famous concert hall, which helped musicians to arrange their appearances and tours.

I very much enjoyed my work at Ibbs and Tillett. My time in Italy had only increased my love for classical music. I wasn't making much money but I loved meeting the musicians. A famous quartet would often stop by for morning coffee and help me finish my crossword. I was also delighted to take advantage of the job's biggest perk, which was free concert tickets.

There were a couple of moments when I wondered whether I was cut out for a job on Civvie Street, however. The first was when I accidentally posted a musician's passport to the wrong address just as he was about to go on an international tour. I realised almost as soon as I let the envelope drop into the post box. We had to get the post office to agree to open the box up so that I could fish the passport out again. The second time was when a man walked into my office as I was up to my neck in mail that needed to be sent out A.S.A.P. Rather than asking his name and his business, I straightaway suggested that he sit down on a pile of sheet music and help me to lick envelopes, of which there were hundreds to be sealed. He did so without complaint. Once we'd finished the job, I finally asked him who he was. And that was when he told me that he was in fact the owner of the agency. Luckily, he was very good-natured about the whole thing. At least I'd made him a cup of tea for his trouble!

Pat and I tried to meet up whenever we could but her job kept her very busy so we didn't see as much of each other as we would have liked. But there was no doubt that we would both be at Newland Hall when our father came home.

When our father left for Singapore, Bobby and I were still schoolchildren. Pat was home on sick leave from Pearn, Pollinger and Higham, the literary agency. She had yet to join the Wrens. How the few short years that had passed since that day had changed us all. While Daddy had always assumed that we children would go into one or other of the forces, he had no idea how that assumption had panned out. Though our mother had written endless letters, telling him all about life back home, he didn't know that Pat was a Wren and I had joined the FANY. In fact, while he was sailing back to the UK, Daddy was tended by the nurse who had cared for me so kindly after my dramatic fall off the cliff in Italy. When the nurse heard Daddy's name – Colonel Cary Owtram – she told him, "I think I've met your daughter. Name of Jean? She was with the FANY in Italy." Daddy told the nurse she must be mistaken. Why on earth would I have been in Italy? In our father's mind, I was still the young girl helping to catalogue Grandboffin's pedigree dairy herd.

On 12 October 1945, Daddy's ship docked in Liverpool. He had to make a quick official visit to his regiment's headquarters in Blackpool before he could finally come home. We were all at Newland Hall when he arrived at 8.30.

As his car pulled up in front of the house, we waited in the drawing room, excited but nervous. We had no real idea what to expect. Daddy was very tanned and thin, of course, after all those years on short rations, but he was instantly recognisable. He was accompanied by a couple of officials, who seemed to have had a drink or two along the way. One could hardly blame them for celebrating.

I had a Box Brownie camera by now and we took photographs to mark the occasion. There are two. In the first, I'm behind the camera and Pat is by our father's side. In the second, Pat and I have swapped places. Bobby and our mother look radiantly happy. Pops and Grandboffin, our two beloved grandfathers, flank the family, upright and dignified as ever.

Once the euphoria of meeting again after so long was over, we settled down to hear how Daddy had passed the last two years. Our joy at seeing our father safely home (and our delight that he had even managed to buy gifts for us in Bangkok) was of course tempered by thoughts of all those who had not made it back. More than 2,500 men of the 137th had died, meaning that there were not enough survivors to reform the regiment now that they were home. We were all especially sad about Colonel Holme, a good man, devoted to his men to the end.

Our father explained that George Holme's death had meant an instant promotion for him, from Senior Major to Colonel, which meant that when he and his men were captured and transferred to a Japanese POW camp called Chungkai in Thailand, he was appointed as British Camp Commandant. As such, he became the main point of contact between the prisoners and their Japanese guards.

The prisoners of Chungkai were straight away set to work on building the Burma Railway, which would come to be one of the most infamous construction projects in history. More than 60,000 Allied POWs worked on the 258-mile-long railway, which ran from Ban Pong in Thailand to Thanbyuzayat in Burma and included the notorious "Bridge On The River Kwai". It's estimated that as many as 16,000 of those POWs died, earning the railway its sorry nickname, "The Death Railway".

Our father took his role as Camp Commandant very seriously. He cared not only for the physical welfare of the 8,000 men in the camp but for their psychological welfare too. He established a sort of camp police force and a camp hospital. He arranged for the sharing of news reports which were received via a hidden wireless set.

If any of his men were too sick to work – dysentery, malaria and malnutrition were rife – our father stood up to the camp guards who insisted otherwise. As far as the Japanese guards were concerned, if a man could stand, he could work. When punishment was meted out in such cases, our father would step in on behalf of the sick prisoner, as was later described in a letter by a fellow camp intern, A.B. Miller, published in the *Lancaster Guardian*. "On many occasions I witnessed him (Cary) receiving brutal beatings for his adamant and steadfast refusals to order sick men out to work on the railway.

"This occurred on so many occasions that eventually even the Japanese accepted the fact that if Cary Owtram said so, then those men were indeed too sick for work. There are many ex-POWs, including myself, who owe their survival to Colonel Owtram."

A.B. Miller also wrote, "One of my own vivid personal memories was of one evening returning to Chung-Kai after an exhausting day on the railway, and joining hundreds of others enjoying an 'impromptu' concert, the 'star item' being Cary Owtram, with his beautiful tenor voice, dressed as the 'Red Shadow' singing excerpts from *The Desert Song*."

True to the Daddy we knew of old – the man who had been dubbed the "Singing Major" by his shipmates on the SS Dominion Monarch – our father arranged entertainments for the men in the camp, even organising the building of a makeshift theatre, complete with drop curtains, footlights and dressing rooms. Our father understood the importance of keeping morale high with concerts and comedy and soon pulled together a proper theatre company, complete with a band, from the talent he found all around him. Thanks to fellow prisoners, like Colonel Leo Britt, who had worked as a producer in the West End and on Broadway, the shows were of a very high standard and drew audiences of thousands of prisoners. Even the Japanese camp guards were fascinated.

There were sporting contests too. Our father kept a diary of his three years in the camp, which he prepared for publication upon his return. In the subsequent book, he described New Year 1945, when the Japanese camp commandant, Lieutenant Kokobo, challenged him to a drinking match. There was no refusing Lieutenant Kokobo. Fearing the consequences otherwise, our father matched Kokobo drink for drink through three bottles of Chinese brandy and the local rice spirit.

Our father wrote, "By this time I was getting to the point where I had to think very hard what I was going to say, and things appeared a bit hazy… I hoped for the best, and taking as firm a grip on my senses as possible, fixed my eyes on Camp Headquarters and made for it. My comrades told me I steered a perfectly straight course, which I find hard to believe… I sank into a deep sleep immediately, which lasted from 3.00pm until 7.00 pm, when considerable concern was felt because I was due to take part in a 'Café Colette' show at 8 o'clock… By this time, of course, the whole camp knew about my session with Kokobo and they flocked to the show to see what effect it had had on me. I remember receiving terrific applause at my entrance on stage. All went well until I missed my cue, much to the delight of the audience. Eventually I did realise the situation and made my exit singing in terrific form. The show was voted a great success!

"These were the sorts of incident which made us all laugh and forget for the moment we were prisoners without a hope of freedom in sight. That was the great joy of our theatre: we were able to forget for a couple of hours and let our minds pass through a veil into another world for a time, a world we remembered from happier days."

Our father took a great risk by keeping a diary during his time at Chungkai. Had the diary been discovered, he would have paid a high price indeed. He went to extraordinary lengths to hide it from the Japanese guards, rolling the pages inside hollow sticks of bamboo, and even at one point burying them in the camp's graveyard, but he believed it was vital to record life in the camp for posterity, both as evidence of Japanese war crimes and lest anyone forget the sacrifice made by so many of his fellows.

Apart from having developed a visceral hatred of the Japanese that he would carry to his grave, our father seemed relatively unscathed by his awful adventure. He was given a long spell of paid leave, during which he dedicated himself to getting Newland Hall's overgrown garden back into shape. A little later he set off around the country visiting those friends and relations who had been as anxious as we were to see him return safe and sound.

One evening, Pat and I met up with him in London for dinner. As we waited in the bar of the Mayfair Hotel, our father suggested that we three have a pre-dinner drink.

"What would you like?" he asked us.

"Whisky," Pat and I suggested simultaneously.

Our father was somewhat taken aback. "Girls drink sherry, not whisky," he said. But Pat and I stuck by our choice. We were not the demure young girls he had left behind when he set sail for Singapore. We had both seen and experienced too much to be treated as such delicate creatures still. He seemed to keep forgetting that I had been an Ensign and Pat was a Chief Petty Officer. We were grown women now. And grown women could drink whisky when they felt like it.

It must have been hard for our father to face so many changes upon his return and at the same time to discover that some things had not changed at all. Though he had been British commandant of the camp at Chungkai, back home at Newland Hall he was still the second son and was expected to defer to Grandboffin in all things, just as had been the case when he left for war in 1941. Sometimes the atmosphere was rather strained but eventually life started to settle down again.

As a family, we were very close and very fond of each other so we found the right balance in the end.

That evening at the Mayfair hotel, our father bought Pat and me those whiskies and we toasted his return once again.

CHAPTER THIRTY-FIVE

Patricia

In November 1945, I left the Wrens. I had a low release date as I was young and had joined late, but by now I was desperately keen to get out. But what would I do next? My godmother Aunt Ellie, who had inadvertently suggested I join Bletchley Park with her observation about the "crowd of jolly girls", had an idea. One which suited me this time.

I was demobilised on a Friday and the following Monday morning, I was on my way to Oslo, to help Aunt Ellie's husband, Uncle Laurence, who had been the Ambassador to Norway since 1940, staff up the British embassy there. I wasn't quite clear what I was going to be asked to do once we arrived. Aunt Ellie thought I was there to be her social secretary. The foreign office saw my official role as that of the embassy's assistant archivist. I hoped to do a lot of skiing.

I flew out to Norway in a converted Dakota. I'll never forget the excitement I felt as I saw the coastline of Great Britain shrinking into the distance behind us. It should have been a relatively short journey but because of bad weather, we had to land in Copenhagen. Luckily, the pilot had some Danish Kroner and he took us passengers out to a restaurant where I ate an oyster for the very first time. We spent one night in Denmark and flew on again the next day.

Aunt Ellie and Uncle Laurence were already in Oslo but as yet had been unable to move into the Embassy as the building still needed some repairs. Several windows had been blown out by the limpet mines the Norwegian resistance had attached to the German ships in the port.

The embassy was in a rather elegant house with a large garden. It had once been the home of the Nansen family. As I was shown around, I remember noticing at once that all the embassy calendars were still showing April 1940, when the Nazis marched in and the Norwegian King and his court escaped with some of the embassy staff via Trondheim to exile in Britain. It was most haunting.

While the embassy was being refurbished, I lived with Aunt Ellie and Uncle Lawrence in a rented house that had been used by the Gestapo during the occupation. The house had a strange, sinister atmosphere and I was very glad when we were able to move out. While we were there, however,

I did enjoy the opportunity to take breakfast with Uncle Lawrence each day. He enjoyed reading the local papers and made me laugh by pointing out how many times the Norwegian journalists used the phrase "beklagelike episode", which meant "lamentable episode", to refer to all sorts of calamities, big and small. "Beklagelike episode" became a sort of catchphrase for us.

In my official civil service role as assistant archivist, I worked alongside Miss Bing, who had been the embassy's archivist at the time the Nazis marched into Oslo. She told me how she and Sir Cecil Dormer, who was the British minister to Norway between 1934 and 1941, had rushed to burn piles of secret files on a brazier in the embassy's garden. Once that was done, Miss Bing and other embassy staff rushed to escape via Sweden, not knowing if she would ever return to Norway again.

Miss Bing kindly showed me the ropes. Among my tasks was to deal with the bags of diplomatic post that arrived several times a week from London, making sure that the letters reached their intended recipients. One letter went astray and was later found stuck in the back of a filing cabinet. You can imagine my dismay when I saw that the letter had come from Buckingham Palace and was supposed to have been delivered to the Norwegian king! Thankfully, the letter itself was not urgent. It was a "thank you" note from Princess Elizabeth for a birthday present. All the same, finding that letter was a heart-stopping moment for me.

Another morning, we opened the door of our office to discover that a burglar had attempted to break in overnight. He'd posted his tools through the letterbox but failed to get through the door himself. We kept the tools, finding they came in very useful whenever we forgot the code to the office safe.

There were still German soldiers in Norway at this time. They were lower rankings, prisoners of war, who were waiting to be moved back to Germany. Pending their journey home, some of them had been assigned to work in the gardens of the embassy, though they never seemed to be doing much work when I saw them. I hated to have to walk by them. They whistled and cat-called as my friends and I passed by. Of course, I could have responded to them in German, but I knew it would have been beneath my dignity to do so. I was pleased when they were moved on.

After a few weeks in Oslo, I was invited with a group of embassy staff to visit the house where Quisling, the infamous Norwegian traitor who had collaborated with the Nazis, had lived during the war. When the country was liberated, Quisling was sent to Germany to face justice there. I took a leaf from a calendar on his desk, 1 January 1945, thinking that no-one would need it now.

Though the memories of the occupation were still fresh, it was a very interesting time to be in Oslo. The Norwegians were delighted to be liberated and there were lots of dances and parties as various embassies were taken out of mothballs and the city celebrated Norwegian festivals and traditions that had been impossible under Nazi rule.

I spent Christmas 1945 with the family of a teacher with whom I was lodging, having moved out of Aunt Ellie and Uncle Lawrence's house. They were extremely kind and generous people but I was somewhat bemused by their Christmas dinner tradition. Instead of the Christmas pudding I was used to, my Norwegian hosts brought out a heap of rice which contained one small piece of pork. They explained that the person who found the pork would be very lucky. I had to agree. It was a very small piece of pork indeed.

On 17 May, Norway's national day, we joined the people of Oslo, many of whom were dressed in national costume, to process past the palace and pay our respects to Haakon VII. Haakon was married to an English woman, Queen Maud. I was lucky enough to meet them on occasion, when Aunt Ellie took me along to the palace when she was visiting her friend, who was a lady-in-waiting there.

Midsummer's Day was another time of great celebration in Norway, celebrated with feast, fireworks and bonfires, and displays of country dancing.

Our embassy often entertained the crews of visiting British ships with parties and tea dances. They were very inclusive occasions. At one particular dance, a navy cadet told me in astonishment, "This morning I was scrubbing the decks. This afternoon I've danced with a Norwegian princess!"

I remember being invited to watch an exhibition of fencing at the French embassy. The invitation described the dress code as "Smoking". I thought it was rather curious but duly turned up in a simple day dress carrying a fresh packet of cigarettes. Upon seeing all the other women in cocktail dresses, I quickly realised that "le smoking" is French for "black tie" and I was entirely underdressed for the occasion. I wouldn't make that mistake again.

But even if I had understood the dress code, I wouldn't have had anything very smart to wear that night. As a Wren, I'd had no need for evening gowns or coupons with which to buy one. Most of the dresses I did have were still stuck in my trunk in transit. I have a series of chits charting the progress of enquiries regarding my delayed luggage. "Where is Owtram's trunk?" Because I was embassy staff, they are all signed "Bevin". Ernest Bevin was the new foreign secretary.

For the moment though, I was in Norway without a dance frock. Aunt Ellie came to the rescue. She took some black velvet which was intended to make curtains and she had a dressmaker use it to run up a long dress for me. It was very elegant, a black velvet dress with a lace trim around the collar. Aunt Ellie provided the lace too. Unfortunately, there wasn't quite enough material for a medium-wide skirt and it was very narrow for dancing. I had to cut in a slit. And when I did dance, I quickly discovered that it was rather hot!

I already felt rather unglamorous compared to the local young women, who were all tall, good-looking and blonde. My curtain dress didn't help! I was sure I had no hope of competing with the Norwegian girls for the attentions of the Scottish soldiers who were based in Oslo at the time, though there was an occasion when a Scottish officer said to me, "I do wish that every conversation with a Norwegian girl didn't start with 'When I was sitting on Grini under the war'…"

Grini was the Nazi concentration camp for political prisoners in nearby Baerum where many of those glamorous girls had spent the war.

Oslo was a very international city at this time. It might have been a backwater were it not for one particular area of expertise. Norway had the capacity to make heavy water, a form of water containing two atoms of the hydrogen isotope deuterium, instead of the protium atoms in ordinary H2O. Heavy water is an essential ingredient in the process of creating atomic weapons and energy. During the war, the Allies had bombed Vermork, the heavy water plant at Rjukan in Norway's Tinn district, thus preventing the Germans from effectively using it for their own atomic experiments. Post war, governments from all over the world were eager to get their hands on heavy water again.

I once came across the Vermork plant while cross-country skiing. Of course, civilians couldn't get close enough to see what went on there, but thanks to my having signed the Official Secrets Act and my experience with knowing how to keep important information confidential, I was asked to type up several secret files regarding heavy water that were sent from our embassy to the government back in London.

Although I'd been horrified when the Americans dropped atomic bombs on Hiroshima and Nagasaki, at the same time I agreed with my father that those bombs had effectively ended the conflict with Japan. Without them, my father might not have survived the war. I told myself it was unlikely that they would ever be used again.

But the Americans and the Russians were among the nations keen to cut deals for heavy water. The Russian Embassy was opposite the British one and occasionally we would meet their staff at events. I remember that one of them made a particularly strong impression on me. He was from Siberia and when he smiled, he revealed a gleaming set of steel teeth. He looked like the character Jaws from the 1970s Bond films, *Moonraker* and *The Spy Who Loved Me*.

I took advantage of everything Norway had to offer. I quickly made several local friends, who helped me to polish my Norwegian language skills. The embassy provided lunches for junior chancery staff such as myself at a nearby house where I met some of the sisters from the Red Cross hospital, who invited me to go skiing with them at weekends.

In the spring of 1946, I attended the reopening of the enormous ski jump just outside the city. It was a big day for Norway and the daring feats of the jumpers took my breath away. I had not learned to ski as a child but I quickly got the hang of cross-country skiing and took the opportunity to practise whenever I could. We would go to the ski fields between Oslo and Bergen. My friends taught me how to know when I needed to "be a herring", which referred to going forward in a straight line, or "be a crab", which meant to tackle a piece of ground sideways on. I even got to try ski-jumping, on small ramps which we built for ourselves.

How I loved the Norwegian countryside. A couple of times I took the train to see friends who lived on the line to Sweden. Their town was so remote that one had to make a special request for the train driver to stop there. They came to meet the train in a pony and trap. That last part of the journey, sitting in the trap under fur blankets as the pony trotted through the snow, felt like stepping into the pages of Tolstoy's *Anna Karenina*.

One of the Red Cross sisters to take me under her wing was Solveig Rønnig, who became a life-long friend.

Solveig was from Trondheim, 300 miles due north of Oslo. I once went with her to visit her family farm. While we were out walking, we stopped to talk to a farmer, whom Solveig knew. He invited us into his hut, telling me, "I've got something from England to show you." I expected to see a Union Jack or something like that. In fact, what he wanted to show me was an English-made machine gun. He'd been a resistance fighter during the war and the gun had been part of an ammunition drop by the Brits.

The mountainous terrain of Norway made resistance easier than it was, say, for the citizens of Denmark, which is a much flatter country. I heard many stories about the resistance, including one of a young resistance fighter who was bicycling to Bergen when he came upon a German patrol. He was stopped and the German soldiers asked him what was in his rucksack.

"Oh you know," he laughed. "A couple of hand grenades and some ammunition…"

The Germans laughed with him, thinking that no-one would joke about such things if he really had grenades and ammunition in his bag. They let him go on his way. Of course, he really was carrying those hand grenades.

At a party in July 1946, I met one of Norway's biggest heroes – Max Manus. Manus was a famous resistance fighter and one of the most brilliant saboteurs of WWII. He'd fought during the unsuccessful Norwegian Campaign then joined the underground movement, helping to distribute illegal propaganda, sourcing weapons and making bombs. After he took part in a plot to assassinate Himmler and Goebbels while they were in Oslo, Manus found himself on the Gestapo's most wanted list and was captured. However, because he was injured during his arrest, he was taken to the Oslo hospital rather than a prison. From there he was able to escape to Sweden and embark upon a long journey via Russia, Turkey, the Middle East and South Africa to get to the United States. There he trained with the Norwegian military in exile before being sent to Scotland to hone his sabotage skills.

Parachuted back into Oslo, he set to work with a team of similarly trained saboteurs to sink German ships in the Oslo Fjord with home-made limpet mines. His work was very important and after the war he was recognised with Norway's War Cross with Sword. He was also recognised by the British with the Distinguished Service Order and the Military Cross and Bar. His investiture took place in the embassy.

I wrote about the encounter at the party, which happened a few weeks later, in my diary, *"Went to a party hosted by Peggy Walker and Siguyst: marvellous food and nice dinner. It lasted from 8 – 1 am and I talked to Max Manus for about an hour – he is nice and easy to get on with and to my surprise had registered seeing me at his investiture at the Embassy in May or June, or earlier. He said he didn't like flying – too scared – and told us about a girl friend who is getting the KM for courage – as her husband's flat was surrounded by 50 Germans and she handed him hand grenades and he shot his way out... Anyway, it was a good party and I MET Max Manus at last."*

The Embassy often welcomed guests from Britain too. In the spring of 1947, I met Malcolm Sargent, the famous British conductor and co-founder of the London Philharmonic, who was in Norway on a concert tour. Sargent was something of a national treasure, familiar to many from his appearances on the BBC Home Service. During the War, he'd continued to tour the country, believing, as our father did, that music was essential for morale. I was thrilled to have a chance to meet him at last and to experience something of his charisma, writing in my diary,

"In the evening went to a concert at the Aula – Malcolm Sargent conducting. Programme was rather interesting – paucity of strings made tone rather squeaky. Sargent worked orchestra as never worked before – beautiful hands. He told story next day at lunch about old lady who asked him 'Tell me, where did you learn your gestures?' – 'Oh well, you know, you just feel the music,' he said, 'and you seem to make the gestures you feel really' 'Oh,' she said. 'But it's so clever of you to keep in time so well!'

Audience walked out as usual immediately concert finished and Sargent said next day how disconcerting it is to turn round and see only retreating backsides as happens in Norway.

"Never known such magnetic vitality, Sargent is dark, elegant, monkey-faced and marvellously lively. Full of racy stories and gets away with it. Put forward outrageous arguments and ribald theories and everyone said Yes, yes, yes, and found themselves suddenly at some point of irrefutable illogic. Sargent said that Grand Hotel let an autograph hunter into his room in early hours of this morning. Was reminded of the time he conducted at Wakefield, Yorks, and in black-out afterwards a girl came up to him and said, 'Are you Dr Malcolm Sargent?'

'Yes.'

'Are you that Dr Malcom Sargent that's on t' Brains Trust?'

'Yes.'

'Then Ah'll 'ave yer autograph.'

Also told us about a visit to Portugal when Mayor of Lisbon came up to him at all-Portuguese party and asked, 'Vous parlez Français?'

'Oui, un peu.'

'Moi,' he said sadly. 'Je ne peux pas.'

Sargent thought it was a good idea to learn these two piquant phrases in all languages and use them on people who couldn't talk whatever language it was (But I think it would leave a more lasting impression to use them, like the Mayor of Lisbon, on people who could.)

Another old lady asked him what it was like to stand on the rostrum conducting. 'Madame,' he said. 'What does it feel like to have a baby?' As she was a respectable old maiden lady she blushed and asked what was the last thing a conductor did before going on to the stage. Sargent, who has a gift for stubbing out people's silly questions, told her that before the war he checked up on his fly buttons – now he goes round his cuffs with a pair of scissors, snip snip snip! And lots more stories. He was interesting… He also gave me his chocolate ration which he isn't allowed to eat."

In the summer I was part of a group, with Solveig, that rented a hut on an island in a lake. There was riding too. When the German officers who had been part of the force occupying Norway were sent back to prison camps in Germany, they were unable to take their horses with them. When the Belgian military attaché discovered what had happened, he looked for a volunteer to ride with him in the mornings. Those horses needed exercising and I was only too happy to help. They were beautiful gentle horses, impressively sure-footed as they crossed the hilly terrain outside Oslo. I felt rather sorry for the officers who had to leave them behind. They must have missed them very much.

From time to time I had visitors. Bob came out to see me during his school holidays. He had a wonderful time. As did Jean. When she visited, we took a side trip to Copenhagen together. Our mother was less impressed. She came out to stay with her cousin, Aunt Ellie, but she looked forward to going back within minutes of having unpacked her case. Jean later told me that even as our mother was getting ready to take her trip to see me – her very first trip overseas – she'd said, "Won't it be nice to get home again?"

Returning to Oslo after showing my mother around, I wrote in my diary: *"On the way back to town was suddenly eaten up with regret at leaving Norway. But in a way I know I must. Am now in Oslo-Bergen train going through heavenly country. Green birches, red-stemmed pines and lichened rocks and the altering blue hills… We are going along the edge of a deep steep dark fjord, among sudden hills. Can imagine Viking skips gliding round such headland!"*

I loved Norway and I was very glad to have the chance to get to know it while I planned my next move.

CHAPTER THIRTY-SIX

Jean

In 1946, I left Ibbs and Tillett to lend my services to a FANY-run organisation dedicated to helping refugees liberated from the concentration camps find homes in the United Kingdom. I was encouraged by Lilly and her friends, who had brought so much to the life of my family when the rise of Nazism chased them away from their homes in Austria.

In the early hours of the morning, I would join my team to go down to the Port of London to meet refugees straight off the ship. They made a pitiful sight, as they disembarked into the damp London morning air, cold and tired and clutching their most treasured belongings. They weren't able to bring much but what they did bring gave me an insight into their fears for the future. Many carried food. Sausages and bread. That sort of thing. One woman refused to let go of a string bag full of bread and fruit that was clearly rotten and would have made her ill had she eaten it. She would not be parted from that rotting food no matter how hard I tried in my best German to convince her that here in England there would be plenty to eat. She simply could not believe it. And why should she? Why should she trust that Britain would be kind to her after her experience of such unkindness at the hands of the Nazis?

The fact that I spoke German came in very useful, both because I was able to explain to the refugees what was going to happen on their arrival and also because I was able to eavesdrop on their conversations to some extent and find out what they *really* thought of the situation. Were they happy to be in England? Were they scared? The more I could find out, the better able I would be to help them.

The pain of the last few years showed in the refugees' faces and of course in the concentration camp tattoos that were an indelible testament to their suffering. Those crudely inked numbers came as a horrible shock to me when I saw them for the first time, reminding me as they did of the way we'd tagged Grandboffin's pedigree cattle. The Nazis had seen these people, their fellow human beings, as animals. That was the horrible truth. I felt sick at the thought of such inhumanity.

I'd had, if there can ever really be such a thing, "a good war". Though of course I was always worried about my father and concerned for Pat and the rest of the family back in England, I myself had not experienced violence. I'd not gone hungry. In Egypt, I didn't even have to worry about rations. It was almost as though I had lived a double life throughout 1944 and 1945. I'd been doing war work but I'd been living in a peacetime atmosphere, where I didn't have to worry about German bombing raids and such. Until I worked with those refugees, I'd really had no idea of the deprivation some people in German-occupied territories had endured. I was glad I could do my small part to help them.

However, it was not easy to find people who were willing to take in a refugee family. Many people in Britain, and especially London, felt they had already given enough. They'd sent their sons and daughters off to war and lived through the Blitz. We were all still existing on rations. Now they just wanted to try to get back to the normal lives they'd been living before 1939. Because of this, part of my role was to rally support for our cause and overcome these understandable objections.

I remember the first time I was asked to give a speech to a large group of people. I had no experience in public speaking and if I'd been able to pick my audience, I certainly wouldn't have picked the room full of businessmen before me. I felt very nervous indeed as I stepped up to the lectern and began to talk. It was terrible. A couple of minutes in, I was ready to pick up my notes and make a run for it.

My audience sat in complete silence. You could have heard a pin drop and I was sure I had bored them to death! I carried on all the same. Perhaps it was being so nervous that made me press on with more and more emotion in my voice. I owed it to Lilly and Edith, who had looked after me so well when I was a child, to at least finish presenting my argument.

As I ended my speech, I was taken by surprise when the audience suddenly burst into applause. I hadn't been boring the businessmen after all. They had been listening with genuine concern and interest and now they wanted to know what they could do to help. Later, a local newspaper reported my speech, saying, "Miss Owtram gave an impassioned plea." I was both astonished and delighted that it had worked. It turned out to be one of my most successful meetings.

Once people heard about the plight of the refugees, once they'd listened to some personal stories and had been told what they could do to alleviate the situation, more and more were willing to offer their help and even open up their homes.

The longer I worked with the refugees, the more I came to realise that the best way to help them settle into their new homes and lives was by approaching everything in a laid-back manner. For example, the last thing they needed was to be rushed straight from the ship to a train to a meeting with a mayor and the members of a local council, all eager for a photo opportunity, as often happened at the beginning.

Likewise, we had to tell the families with whom the refugees had been billeted that their good intentions, in the form of welcoming parties and dinners with the neighbours, might be overwhelming. The English way of life can be hard to understand even when you're born here.

The children seemed to make connections more easily than the adults. They were perhaps more resilient. They were better able to pick up a new language and quickly absorb a new culture. As it was, many of the refugees I met and got to know were not planning to stay long in England anyway. England was just a stepping stone. Most of them had their sights set on America, where the European Jews who had left before the war had established thriving communities, and where there were greater opportunities than could be found in tired-out, war-weary Britain.

It wasn't only the refugees who wanted to move on to pastures new. I had realised pretty much as soon as I returned to England that I wanted to be back on the Continent. In Italy, in particular. But how?

Though the country had turned its back on Winston Churchill in the 1945 general election, Fitzroy Maclean had survived re-election as the MP for Lancaster. In January 1947, I decided, given our connection through Lancaster and my time in Italy supporting agents in the Baltics, that

I would write to him and see whether there was any way he could help me to get another job overseas. He responded almost at once by telephone.

"Can you type?" he asked.

"Yes."

"Shorthand?"

"Yes."

"Have you got a passport?"

"Of course," I said.

'Then I'll see you on Monday morning. Lancaster station. Half past nine."

He was taking me with him to Italy. I couldn't wait to go back.

War Office Special Mission
c/o H Q Allied Commission
CMF
2nd February 1947

My darling Mummy and Daddy,

Well, here we are! We got here at breakfast time yesterday after a simply wonderful and very comfy journey. I called and telegraphed etc. from various points – I hope you got everything. We left London at 8.20am on Thursday from Victoria and had breakfast on the train. London last week was so cold it just couldn't be described! We got to Dover about 11 and went straight on board after going through the customs. The boat was about the size of the Bretagne and brand new – very comfy and a lovely lunch at 11.30! It was a glassy smooth crossing, although there was half a gale blowing and you couldn't stand up in the bows. It must have been a very steady boat, I imagine. We landed at Calais soon after 1 and were shepherded onto a train with reserved seats waiting so we didn't have to organise anything ourselves. We had tea on that train – rusks, jam and tea without sugar or milk. I imagine that's the usual French standard as meals on our next train, the Simplon-Orient Express, were very different.

We got to Paris after dark unfortunately, and crossed to the Gare de Lyons in taxis. It was very well lit and looked adequately gay and civilised, but we didn't see very much of it. I sent off my cable from the station (my French getting worse every moment!) and we also had supper there in the buffet. The next train was lovely. We had two-bunk cabins – Jean and I shared – and a very good dining car. The Maclean children spent a lot of time with us and we both developed latent talent for telling stories by the time we got to Italy! We reached the Swiss frontier about midnight but being diplomatic didn't have to go through the customs – our Admin. Officer John Selby (a Group Captain from Bari) dealt with everything, poor thing. I was asleep when we went through Lausanne, and when I woke up around 6.30 we were right in the Alps. Lovely snowy *mountains and dove-coloured sky, with conventional grey stone chalets and dry brown grass. It wasn't nearly as snowy as England or, later, Milan.*

We turned east at Martigny and went up the Rhone Valley to Brig, through a little town called Sion. Most of the mountains round here were white, as we were climbing all the time. At Sion the sun came up and touched the crests of the mountains, and the snow turned pink and gold. At Brig we turned south again and went through the Simplon tunnel. It's the longest in the world and took half an hour to go through. At the other side we dropped down very quickly to Domodossola through rocks and green rivers and mountains. From there we went down the side of Lake Maggiore, very cold and grey with islands packed to the water with red-roofed houses, to Milan, where we had a wait for long enough to send off a postcard to you. We went from there to Bologna where we had a vast Italian dinner on the train and on through Florence to Rome. It was wonderful to get back and recognise places and hear Italian again.

We're living in the Hotel Continental in the Via Cavour, which is a big modern hotel taken over for the army and its wives and children. Jean and I share a reasonably large room with a private bathroom of the same size. The food is very good and we really are living in great luxury! The Macleans and a Col. Vivien Street and his wife and baby are in the Grande, about five minutes' walk away. We all collected there last night to be told about the work. It sounds frightfully interesting and quite exciting, though goodness knows how we've to get through it in six months. It's still pretty secret so I can't tell you any details – if anyone asks say we're just finding out which of the DPs are eligible for help from the IRO (the International Refugee Organisation) which is, after all, exactly what we are doing, with trimmings.

Jean and I spent this morning walking around Rome looking at shops and things. There's so much to buy I can see my princely pay melting overnight. Perhaps fortunate from the point of view that I'm on the party that goes off to camps to interview the DPs. I'm frightfully pleased about this as it's by far the most interesting job of the lot. Eight of us go – five officers and a girl called Gwen Lees who was a FANY with me in Cairo and very nice and whose husband is among the officers, and another ex-FANY called Gwen (!) Buxton, and me. For the first trip we are also taking John Selby and a Major called Stephen Clissold to look around and see how things go to report back to Fitzroy in Rome. Clissold was a journalist in Belgrade before the war, and an agent there during it and has written some books on the Partisans etc. so is clearly very knowledgeable about this job! All the others are also picked for their previous experience of Yugoslavia and the Balkans generally and are a very good team indeed, and all wildly enthusiastic, which is such fun and so much better than the usual bored War Office people. They were

*nearly all in the field as agents during the war and know Bari
and the people I do, so I have rather a privileged position! I'm
longing to get started.*

*How is Pops going on? I do hope it isn't so painful now
and he is much more himself. Do give him my very best love and
much sympathy. Also my love to Grandboffin and Bob and Lilly,
to all of whom I will write when I'm a bit more organised – I'm
writing on my knee at present in the bedroom, which is why this
is so illegible.*

With lots and lots of love,
Jane

*P.S. Among six secretaries there are three Jeans and two Gwens
so I am becoming Jane instead!*

It was quite the journey. For the most part, while we were in
Rome, I worked as a personal assistant to Maclean's deputy.
My duties were mostly secretarial. The shorthand and typing
skills I'd picked up at the Triangle College got plenty of use.
From time to time, I also helped take care of the Maclean
children, particularly the new baby. It was a far cry from my
coding work but I enjoyed it all the same.

In Italy with the FANY, I had blossomed. When I got to
Rome with the Maclean mission, it was exactly as wonderful

as I remembered. Throughout my life, I have retained that love for Italy and the Italians. I spent as much time there as I could. What heaven it was to be back.

CHAPTER THIRTY-SEVEN

Jean

After a short period in Italy, the mission took me to Austria, where I worked to help more displaced people find new homes.

The horror of the Nazi regime was brought home to me in the most visceral way in Austria, when I visited Mauthausen. Mauthausen was a market town not far east of the city of Linz, on the banks of the Danube. Since Roman times, it had been an important stopping-off point on the trade routes across Europe.

There was a prisoner of war camp at Mauthausen during the First World War. Of the 40,000 Italian, Russian and Serbian prisoners who were kept there, more than a quarter died. So perhaps the people of Mauthausen were already hardened to the idea of the industrialisation of death when the Nazis set up one of their first concentration camps three miles to the west of the town.

Mauthausen was chosen because it was close to a quarry. In 1938, after the annexation of Austria, the SS had created a company called German Earth and Stone Works, to extract stone using the labour of prisoners. 300 Austrian prisoners were transported from Dachau to build the Mauthausen camp. They were forced to carry granite blocks up the 186 steps of what would become known as the "Stairway to Death".

To begin with, the prisoners at Mauthausen comprised mostly convicted criminals and people the Nazis deemed "asocial" but by 1939, the camp had grown from 300 to 2,600 and included Jehovah's Witnesses and conscientious objectors. Soon they were joined by Spanish Republicans, refugees from the Civil War who had been turned over to the Nazis by France's Vichy Government. By the time the camp was liberated, almost 200,000 prisoners had been registered there. They included 14,000 Jewish people, 37,000 non-Jewish Poles, 23,000 Soviet civilians, more than 8,000 Yugoslavians, 6,000 Italians, 4,000 Czechs and 47 Allied servicemen, who were all agents of the SOE.

The contrast between Mauthausen's pretty tourist town face and the hell of the camp was shocking. Thanks to the testimonies of survivors, we now knew exactly what had gone on inside those walls, just a short walk from the beautiful Danube.

As the train arrived at the station, it hit me. There were two platforms. As a tourist, you stepped off in one direction. As a prisoner of the Nazis, you would have stepped off in the other and walked in the direction of certain death.

I was taken inside by a guide and seeing how low the walls were, I asked why no-one had tried to escape. Surely they could have climbed out? But of course, even a low wall is high enough when a gun is being trained on you and you're weak and you're tired because you haven't eaten properly for months.

In the underground prison cells, I saw piles of the striped pyjamas the prisoners had worn and piles of battered boots and shoes. There were hundreds and hundreds of pairs, many of which were small enough to have belonged to children.

I had seen photographs of such piles of shoes and clothes and pairs of glasses and hairbrushes, but nothing had prepared me for seeing them in situ. They were such personal, human things.

That the camp was now empty of people somehow made it all the more real and more shocking. Mauthausen was horrific beyond relief. It's estimated that less than 20 percent of the people who were taken to Mauthausen survived their incarceration. As I walked the paths made by their forced labour, the ghosts of those who didn't make it out alive were everywhere.

The War Crimes Commission were still hunting down war criminals who needed to be brought to trial. Of course, as we now know, many of the most senior and most evil members of the regime escaped justice by fleeing to South America. However, many others were tracked down and arrested and after my shocking visit to Mauthausen, I was able to see the trial of a number of men who had worked there.

A friend who was working on the trial had a number of tickets to sit in the gallery and he gave one to me. Having seen the devastation these people had wreaked, I wanted to see them get their just desserts. All the same it was a peculiar feeling to be sitting just a few feet away from them in a court room, breathing the same air.

Until that day, I don't think I had ever really encountered true evil. The first man to be marched into the court looked disarmingly ordinary but as the second defendant was brought in, I swear I could actually feel it. I knew I was in the presence of evil then. I felt the prickle of goosebumps all over my body as I looked at his face. This was not a man who had merely been following orders. He had believed in what he was doing and his aura was almost inhuman. As his eyes grazed the faces of the people in the public gallery I shrank away from his gaze.

Later, I wrote about the Mauthausen trial in a letter to my parents.

Special Refugee Commission
c/o H C B T A
Austria GMF
3rd September 1947

My darling family,

...Today was a half day and I spent most of it in a War Crimes trial. We have a small Nuremberg going on in K just now and fortunately I know several members of the War Crimes Group and they got me a pass to go and listen. They're trying 12 men who were connected with the biggest Austrian concentration camp, at Mauthausen (it had a 90% death rate). Workers were drawn from there to build a tunnel through the Loibl Pass a few miles south of here, which connects Yugoslavia and Austria. We've got 22 Frenchmen staying in the hotel, who were working there, and who have come back to give evidence. I've been intro-duced to the leader, Louis Something, who was working in the underground in Paris in 1940, before we'd learned any of the things we knew later, and was picked up in '42, spent five months in solitary confinement, and then 3 years in this camp. Talking to individuals it seems incredible that they're still sane and amusing and normal, but in the court it becomes so impersonal. You never feel it has to do with the people in front of you at all.

The 12 prisoners are pure Hollywood but far worse. They all look completely devoid of any reasonableness — most of them look mad. The two worst are the doctor and the commandant, Winkler. Winkler was a gardener in an asylum before he was given Mauthausen. The doctor did all the things one reads about in the Sunday dispatch, but it's frightfully hard to believe one's looking at a real person, while the witnesses tell about him. It's as if anything so evil automatically became inhuman. He came from a very good family and was very intelligent too and there isn't even the excuse of sheer uneducated brutality that the others have. Winkler is definitely mad and doesn't seem to take much in. Then there's one called Sachs who is absolutely square – square head, heavy hair, square jaw and heavily built. I don't think he's got enough brain to be mad – just cruel. And Max, who has fair hair that looks as if it's been permed and a queer-shaped face and pale eyes, and who is supposed to have been one of the worst under-officers. And a tall thin one called Preiss or Griess or something, who has the coldest face I've ever seen – just frozen hate of everyone and so on. Each worse than the last, except for one known as Uncle Franz, for whom one of the Frenchmen put in a good word because he had once let him go to the labby when the commandant had forbidden it, and had given him half a cigarette to smoke inside. And I felt that if after two or three years he still remembered it as being important enough to put against the evidence against Uncle Franz, who was being tried for his life, it gave one rather a clear picture of conditions at the time.

It was all rather impressive and calm and remote and very fair. Any point that could be made for the defence, was. The trial is being held in English, German and French, which slows things up rather. The French interpreter is quite useless and the German one, who speaks 10 languages and is an English corporal, helps him out when he can't bear it any longer. So does the Bench, which is also tri-lingual, so it really seems hardly necessary to have the interpreter at all!

The Dr has a very clever young German lawyer to defend him, a well-known Nazi, but not shut up as he is far too clever to have anything pinned down on him, and who has been having terrific parties all week with the prosecutor − an English Major. But all the defending council have no hesitation in letting each other down at every turn − at present they're all trying to push responsibility onto Winkler, but failing him anyone else will do. Presumably they know it's hopeless and most of them will get a death sentence anyway so it doesn't matter what they say. It was all frightfully interesting but rather frightening and subduing.

It's rapidly nearing midnight so I think I must go bye-byes. A very happy birthday for darling Dadda, if this arrives in time, and thank you all most awfully for your letters − I never do any serious work in the mornings till the post has come!

With fondest love darlings.
Jane.

The moment when the witness told the court that he remembered the guard giving him a cigarette was particularly
poignant. What little things count for kindness in war?

It was a very depressing experience but there were happier
times in Austria to come. About ten years after the war ended,
I would go to Vienna as a guest of Lilly and her family.

I was there for three weeks. I spent my days getting to
know the city with one of Lilly's nephews, who was an actor,
as my guide. We took a ride on the kind of carousel that Lilly
had described to us as we sat in the kitchen at Newland Hall.
During the evenings, we often gathered around the piano.
The family was very musical. The young nephew who had
been recognised as a talented violinist as a child was now first
violin with the Vienna Philharmonic.

The Getzls found my attempts at German most amusing.
In fact, I noticed that everyone I met in Austria seemed to find
my attempts at German amusing. Eventually, Lilly explained
the reason. I had been addressing everyone I met using the
familiar "du". Like French, German has two ways of saying
"you" singular, and one is more "proper" than the other. While
everyone understood what I was trying to say, such informality
raised eyebrows when I was talking to the bus driver!

The Getzl family were very kind, open and generous
people. They had suffered terrible losses at the hands of Nazi
Germany. On the way to Vienna by train, as she crossed

Germany, Lilly refused to step out of the carriage, even for a moment, on German soil. One of Lilly's older sisters and that same sister's husband had died in the camps. Another Getzl cousin had spent time in both Dachau and Auschwitz and been forced on a death march. He survived, but the scars of such atrocities would take a long time to heal.

Only slowly were Vienna and her people rebuilding themselves. But seeing the city through the eyes of Lilly's young nephew, it felt as though one day all might be well again.

CHAPTER THIRTY-EIGHT

Patricia

The War changed the lives of so many people. The pain suffered by those who lost their loved ones on both sides was incalculable. So many lost their homelands too. Though she would make the trip to Vienna to see her relatives from time to time, Lilly never returned to live in the city she'd called home. It was too full of painful memories. Lilly had become a dear friend to all of us and stayed on at Newland Hall for many years. One of her relatives recently suggested that Lilly found her true home in England. The English way of being suited her. Though she had grown up in Austria, she was, he said, an English woman at heart. I will always be grateful for the way meeting Lilly changed the trajectory of my life.

Had the War not broken out as Jean and I were getting ready to leave school, who knows what we might have done with our lives? The expectations for women of our social class were rather boring. A secretarial job followed by marriage and motherhood perhaps? The opportunity to go to university certainly wasn't a given, as it might have been for our brother.

While I was in Norway, I met the son of the consul, who was visiting the embassy during the summer holidays. He was a student at St Andrews. He told me how much he loved it there and encouraged me to apply. I knew I didn't want to be a civil servant forever, so I took his advice. I was able to get an Ex-Service Grant and in the September of 1947, I went to University of St Andrews to read English Language and Literature.

I loved being at university. While at St Andrews, I threw myself into student life. I convened debates and edited the university magazine. I wrote several poems, which were published (two of which appear at the end of this book), and graduated with first-class honours. From St Andrews I went on to take a B. Litt at Somerville College, Oxford, focussing my thesis on a 17th-century manuscript, the prompt book of a play. From Somerville, I went to Harvard University for a year on an English-Speaking Union's exchange programme. I graduated from Harvard with an A.M. in English.

After that, I felt it was time to leave academia and find work as a journalist, as had always been my intention. I had been offered a job in New York but I wanted to be an English journalist and also worried that a career in America would mean hardly ever seeing my family. I turned down a position on a magazine in London because the wages were too low. Then my father remembered that he had been at school with the man who was the current editor of the *Daily Mail*. Getting in touch, he discovered that the *Daily Mail* in Manchester was looking for a woman reporter. I applied and won the job.

At around this time, Granada Television was setting up in Manchester too. I wrote some scripts for them freelance before being offered a job as a researcher and news reporter. From there, I moved into television production, working at first on children's and educational programmes before joining the department producing programmes for adults. My knowledge of German still occasionally came in useful. It meant that I was able to liaise directly with the German hospital on the night of the 1958 Munich Air disaster, in which eight members of the Manchester United football team lost their lives. The whole city was on tenterhooks as we waited to hear the latest news. Thankfully, there were 21 survivors, including Bobby Charlton, who would go on to play in the 1966 World Cup winning England team.

In 1962, I was one of the producers of the first series of *University Challenge* with Bamber Gascoigne in the question master's chair. Two years later, I relocated to London to work with the BBC, who were recruiting producers for BBC2, and to be closer to Ray Davies, the man who would become my husband. Ray was a radio reporter who also wrote scripts for Morecambe and Wise's radio show.

I worked on several quiz shows during the course of my career, including *The Biz Quiz*, *Give Me Your Word* and *Ask The Family*, which I created. I also produced *The Sky At Night* series with Patrick Moore for nine years. He and I became very good friends. We flew to Houston together to cover the moon landings in 1969. It didn't escape my notice that the moon landings were made possible by the technology the Germans had developed for their V2s. Later, I arranged for Patrick to interview Neil Armstrong in London. Their conversation was fascinating as they were both much more interested in the moon itself than in the cost of the NASA expedition, which seemed to have been the focus of some of the US press conferences. I also travelled with Patrick to Africa to see an eclipse. If only I could have gone back in time and told my younger self at Newland Hall how life would turn out.

As the years wore on, the war loomed less large in all our lives. People didn't want to think about it anymore. When our father tried to publish his POW camp diaries in the 1950s, he was told that people didn't want to be reminded of those dark days. It was very disappointing for our father to have such a life-changing experience dismissed in that way and, most importantly, not to be able to commemorate the courage of the Far East Prisoners of War as he wanted to do.

It was a long time before Jean and I felt able to share our own war stories even with each other. In fact, it wasn't until the 1960s that we finally sat down and revealed everything – or nearly everything – that we'd been involved in during those heady years between 1942 and 1945.

At the height of the war, the Y stations collected and passed on more than 3,000 messages a day to Station X – Bletchley Park. It was an invaluable contribution to the war effort, if it largely went unsung. Talking about Bletchley and the listening service after the war, Winston Churchill called the people who worked there the "geese that laid the golden eggs but never cackled". We Y station Wrens took that Official Secrets Act very seriously indeed.

Being a Y Service Wren had taught me the importance of being able to keep a secret. Ever since, I've been careful to be discreet and never betray a confidence. Gradually, in the 1970s, information about wartime intelligence began to be declassified, but when various people started to publish their memoirs about their work at Bletchley I thought at first that it was a terrible mistake. Those of us Wrens who were still in touch expressed our dismay to one another.

But now I think that it's important that everything we know about WWII is documented and explained. In 2016, Jean and I were finally able to get our father's diaries published as *1000 Days On The River Kwai: The Secret Diary of a British Camp Commandant*. And now Jean and I tell people what we ourselves did during the war so that they can better understand what a complex undertaking defeating Hitler and the Axis Powers really was and how many different roles were involved. In particular, it's important to highlight the role of women in delivering that final victory.

I'm very pleased that I've had the chance to share my wartime experiences with younger generations through school visits and talks. I'm sure they're surprised when they find out what life was like for a teenage interceptor in the Y service. I talk to older groups too, such as the University of the Third Age. It usually raises a laugh when I tell them that I may be the only old lady in Chiswick who knows how to use a Sten gun.

I was thrilled to be awarded the Legion d'Honneur at the French Embassy in June 2019. Also last year, to my delight, I gave a radio interview in fluent German. I was amused to learn that, according to the interviewer, almost 80 years after I learned to speak the language in the kitchen with Lilly, I still have a slight Viennese accent.

CHAPTER THIRTY-NINE

Jean

I remember when Pat and I finally told each other about our war work. It was during the 1960s. We were having dinner together. As Pat told me about the Y service, I felt very proud of my big sister. She listened with interest as I told her about the agents whose messages I had coded in Cairo, in Italy and at the SOE.

But even in the 1960s, there were still things we didn't know. The fact is that because secrecy was key, even when it came to our own work, we weren't allowed to see the bigger picture. Thus we had very little idea how important our work really was or whether we were succeeding in our aims. In the 60s we still didn't know about the importance of the Enigma code messages Pat had transcribed with such care. For my own part, it wasn't until just three years ago, when I found myself reading about the incident in someone else's book, that I realised just how important that late night message about the "cricket match" was.

Once the Armistice was signed, the Yugoslavs had started racing north to reclaim Trieste from the Italians, just as Tito had said he would back when he and Maclean were planning Operation Ratweek back in August 1944. The "cricket match" was a way of ensuring enough Allied soldiers were already in the city to head off any trouble when the Yugoslavs got there. It worked. Tito was unable to claim the city. For years afterwards, he would refuse to visit Italy as he continued to smart over the loss. It made me wonder what might have happened had I decided that message wasn't worth sending. How many other messages had I sent without understanding how critical they really were and how they might have altered the course of history?

As I look back over my nine and a half decades, being a member of the FANY during the Second World War still feels to me about the most important time of my life. During those two years, I grew up. Though I was 18 and had spent a year at secretarial college, I really was not much more than a schoolgirl when I embarked on my basic training in the Cotswolds. During my time at Baker Street, in Egypt and in Italy, I became an adult. The FANY gave me freedom. I found my independence and gained a degree of self-confidence that would serve me well for the rest of my life. When I came home from Italy in 1945, I felt that I could cope with just about anything. I could adapt to living anywhere. I had the feeling that I could handle whatever life threw at me without being nervous or scared. Confidence. In one word, that's what the FANY experience meant to me.

That confidence served me well in my later career. After working with various refugee missions throughout the 1950s – work that took me all over the globe – in the 1960s I became involved with the setting-up of the brand new University of Lancaster. When I was asked to create a careers department, I did wonder how I could be of any use – I didn't have a degree myself – but I harnessed the spirit of the FANYs to build a careers advice centre that worked just as well for those students who were destined to fail their degrees as well as the high-flyers. There was a little bit of secrecy involved too, as I liaised with the government departments that recruited for the intelligence service. I'd become one of those "women with a purpose" whom I'd professed to despise back in 1945!

It was while working at the University of Lancaster that I met my husband Mike, who was a librarian. I married late. I was already in my forties, as was Pat when she married her husband Ray. Perhaps the taste of independence we'd had during World War Two shaped our decision not to settle early on, and to choose husbands who would understand our need to work and have a full and exciting life outside the home. Mike and I had a wonderful life together. We set up home together in a small Lancashire village and travelled whenever we could.

Of course it would have been better had the war never happened. Through my work with refugees, I learned first-hand about the immense pain and sadness the Nazis had caused. But from a personal point of view, the Second World War shaped my life in a very good way. Were I to have my life over again, I would sign up for the FANY in a heartbeat. When I was born, a girl from my class was destined to live a very narrow existence, focused on husband and children. The war gave me the chance to seek broader horizons and have bigger adventures and I believe that I've been more useful to the world than I might otherwise have been because of it.

The process of writing this book has brought back many memories – some happy and some painful – and raised many questions as well. One of the biggest is whether we should have gone to war against Germany at all? Had it all been worth it, the terrible devastation and the loss of life on both sides?

It goes without saying that all wars are the most terrible calamity and usually probably not necessary, but we regard the Second World War as having been absolutely necessary. Hitler and his Fascist allies like Mussolini had to be stopped. The Nazis were like a great black cloud over Europe. They had to be defeated.

As the 75th anniversaries of both VE Day and VJ Day approach, the lessons of World War Two are still important. As King George VI said in his VJ Day broadcast, which meant so much to us as a family, "relief from past dangers must not blind us to the demands of the future... Great, therefore, is our responsibility to make sure by the actions of every man and every woman here… that the peace gained amid measureless trials and suffering shall not be cast away."

We sisters don't remember meeting anybody during our time in the women's services who had the slightest doubt that we were doing the right thing. We certainly didn't doubt it at all.

Patricia and Jean Owtram

The following poems, inspired by World War Two, were written for the University of St Andrew's magazine in 1949.

LAMENT FOR A CITY
By Patricia Owtram

"… This town was largely destroyed by the Germans
during the war: but people continued to live among
the rubble."

When it was over and there was nothing else to do,
We went back by the same road again,
But slowly, for now we were going home. Old
Wide children's eyes saw tilted tanks, and men
Curiously sprawled, their flesh turned back like silk
Or licked to blackness by a petrol-flame
Or wastefully spilled in broken glass and sand
To thread a dark moss-pattern between the stones;
Everything crazily slanted and twisted, metal
Creased like a petal in a hard hot hand.

But this was only the beginning, and could not harm us
Who carried sorrow heavily under the heart
Towards our city. This was a stranger's pain
Quickly forgotten; and now there was nothing to say
Because we were going home.
    And so we came
To the edge of the town, home.

Everything tilted and rocked and canted
Where sourly the seed of Death was planted
And shot sharp upward blades
Between our houses flung in barricades
Across our streets. And all Spring's alchemy
Would not renew again the red rose tree
Or the vine beside the door.

This was a new way that our garden grew.

And because there was nothing else to do
We came to terms with Death, and so have found
A way to build a city underground
Where the steep sun of noonday never falls
But only half-light crumbles in all day.
And about the shells and shards of broken walls
And under desolate arches, children play
With tattered toys of steel.

....

But this is hardest of all for the heart to learn —
That all things have not changed.
      We should have seen

Nothing that was before, nothing the same
As we had known. Ashlars fresh to the hand
Should have built our city again; but not the worn
Familiar unfamiliar thresholds, torn
And scattered and yet the same. And every stone
Cries out to us, I am your past, yourself…
And we are the ghosts.

O, this we should not have known.

GOLD IS FOR GRIEVING

By Patricia Owtram

I did not know before
    gold was for grieving,
with a tatter of small clouds blown
    across the brittle sky,

with the hoarse barren cry
    of geese gone out beyond a pale shore
to the waste of the sea.
    (O, the pain of their land-leaving.)

Gold slants the sun now,
    gold the trees' weaving
About fields that are brown, brown,
    ridged with the first rime.

O wild skein wheeling,
    strong wings sun-gilded, about the fair sky,
your long seeking done now
    cry to the land that gold's a deceiving,

a loveliness stealing
    from aching air and still sea
at the whisper of time.
    O cry, this is for grieving.

Acknowledgements

We would especially like to thank Chris Manby, for all her hard work and skill in preparing this book. We are also very grateful to Simon Robinson for his endless support and his vital contribution to the book's research and promotion. We'd like to thank our agent David Riding at MBA and our editor Ajda Vucicevic and the team at Mirror Books. Also to Maribel Seno and Claire Burrows, for their invaluable practical support in London and Lancashire.